Dude Ranching with the Walter Family

Irene Knapp
and
Doreen Sloan

This book is a work of non-fiction. Unless otherwise noted, the author and the publisher make no explicit guarantees as to the accuracy of the information contained in this book and in some cases, names of people and places have been altered to protect their privacy.

© 2005 Irene Walter Knapp and Doreen Walter Sloan. All Rights Reserved.

No part of this book may be reproduced, stored in a retrieval system, or transmitted by any means without the written permission of the author.

First published by AuthorHouse 05/16/05

ISBN: 1-4208-5135-7 (sc)

Printed in the United States of America
Bloomington, Indiana

This book is printed on acid-free paper.

Many thanks to our daughter and niece,
Jane, for her work in putting our
thoughts and words into this work.

Thank you also to Pam, Mary,
Waynette, Rene, Jim, Jonathan Potter,
and Pat Hults for their help and support.
Sincere thanks and appreciation to Tracy
for her work on the cover.

~ Irene and Doreen

Table of Contents

Introduction	- 1 -
Preface	- 4 -
The Walter Famil	- 5 -
Dude Ranch Dictionary	- 9 -
Cimarron Guest Ranch	- 13-
Cinnabar Ranch	- 33 -
Rodeos	- 58 -
The War Years	- 78 -
Meet the Walter Children	- 85 -
Poetry	- 98 -
Interesting People at the Ranches	- 100 -
Other Ranches	- 114 -
Ski-Hi Ranch	- 115 -
Indian River Guest Ranch	- 118 -
Double U Ranch	- 123 -
Calico Ranch	- 125 -
Walter Ranch	- 136 -
Timberlane Ranch	- 143 -
Calico Ranch	- 150 -
Flying W Ranch	- 151 -
Lost Wilderness Ranch	- 161 -
Au Sable Guest Ranch	- 163 -
C.J. Ranch Rodeo	- 170 -
Brochures, Newsletters, Memorabilia	- 172 -

Introduction

Join us in sharing our memories
of the ranches with you ...
Irene Knapp and Doreen Sloan

We would like to welcome you to the wonderful world of dude ranching, just as our father would have all those years ago, with a big smile and a warm heart. Step inside these pages and take a ride back to a simpler time. We'll show you how much fun it is to be a dude! Whether it is relaxing by the lake, enjoying a trail ride or thrilling to a rodeo, you are sure to have a great time. We invite you to saddle up and join us at the ranch.

In 1931, Vern Walter, along with his wife, Lu, and his brother Loren, started Ski-Hi dude ranch in Athol, New York. This was the beginning of an exciting chapter in the life of the Walter family.

Preface

The Walter family started one of the earliest Dude Ranches in New York in 1931 and for over thirty years, owned and managed some of the finest vacation spots in the East. The first ranch, Ski-Hi, was opened and operated by Vern Walter in Athol, New York in 1931. Vern then opened Cimarron Ranch in Peekskill, New York in 1939. Allan and C.J. Walter opened the Cinnabar Ranch in Peekskill shortly after in 1940. Throughout the years, the family was also connected to the Indian River Ranch in New Smyrna Beach, Florida; the Calico Ranch in Woodstock, New York; the Walter Ranch in Garrison, New York; the Calico Ranch in Wurtsboro, New York; the Flying W Ranch in Newtown, Connecticut; the Lost Wilderness Ranch in New Boston, Massachusetts; the Au Sable Guest Ranch in Gaylord, Michigan; the Double U Ranch in Tucson, Arizona, and the Timberlane Ranch in East Jewett, New York.

The children of the Walter family grew up in Canada in a lively house full of eleven children, six boys and five girls. We never dreamed of the adventure that awaited us. None of us could have imagined our family growing even larger! When the gates opened to our first dude ranch, our guests made their way onto our ranch and into our hearts. Some guests returned year after year; some never left and became our extended family. Together we made memories and celebrated life.

In writing this book it is our hope that you will experience the warmth of the Walter family and the excitement of the Dude Ranch. Although the Walter family has a rich history with all these ranches, the focus of this story will be on the Cimarron and Cinnabar Dude Ranches in Peekskill, New York.

The Walters in Regina, Saskatchewan, Canada 1939

Top: Kenneth, Vern, Allan, Stan
Below: Earl, George

Connie and C.J. Walter

George and Earl
Maxine, Irene, Doreen
and Jeanette

The Trek East

Connie & C.J.'s Wedding

This is how our story begins. Our mother and father, Connie and Clark, "C.J." Walter, were born in the United States. Their families had migrated to America from England and Norway. After they were married they lived on a small parcel of land in South Dakota. With Mom's small inheritance, she purchased a cow and some chickens, not only to feed her family, but also to market what she didn't need. Our mother was enterprising, and thrifty. She always saved a part of her small income. Our father, C.J., was a dreamer. When he heard he could homestead in Canada, he moved his family up north to where they lived in several small towns in Saskatchewan.

The Walter family had eleven children: Vern, Allan, Stanley, Iona ("Peggy"), Kenneth, Irene, Earl, George, Maxine, Doreen and Jeanette.

Their last move in Canada was to Regina, the capital city of the state. During the depression era, young men couldn't find work. The elder Walter boys, Vern and Allan, left home looking for work in the United States. Brothers Stanley and Kenneth were in college. The oldest daughter, Peggy, went to live in Detroit with Aunt Mae (C.J.'s sister). At home were Earl, George, Irene, Maxine, Doreen and Jeanette. In Canada, our father and mother tried hard to keep the family housed, fed and clothed but it was a struggle. C.J. started his own draying business in Canada. Draying is hauling goods from the train to the customer. He went bankrupt because he couldn't pay a $35.00 loan.

C.J.'s Draying Business

Vern F. Walter, our Dad's younger brother, was born on a ranch near the Badlands of South Dakota. His early ambition was to be a traveling salesman and see the world. He wanted to live in fancy hotels, and wear dude clothes. He started out selling door locks for Ford automobiles. When the Model T Ford was taken off the market he was left jobless and broke, so he decided to start an Eastern Dude Ranch.

He needed a good man to be his corral boss of the Cimarron Guest Ranch in Peekskill, New York.

- 6 -

C.J. Walter

and he asked C.J. if he would take the job. C.J. would be in charge of the horses, rodeo stock, and the guest rides for the summer months.

All his earnings would be sent home to the family. In 1940 the standard wage at the ranches was $30.00 per month, with room and board. It sounded like a good arrangement, so C.J. took off to New York, leaving my mother to cope with their large family. In the fall, when C.J. came home for the winter, he started receiving fan mail from some of the female guests at the ranch. Connie told him that if he were to return to New York, he would need to take the whole family. That is how this wonderful adventure started.

The two last remaining children of this large family, Irene and Doreen, have decided to write this book. Irene is now 81 and her youngest sister Doreen is 73. Doreen has a vivid memory of the ranch years and has supplied most of the information and memories for this book. The pictures of the ranches have been gathered from all members of the family.

The Walter Family

**Top: Earl, George, Allan, Connie, Kenneth, Stan, Vern
Bottom: Peggy, Doreen, Irene, Maxine**

Top: **Doreen, Maxine, Connie, Ingrid, Peggy, Barbara, Guest
Bottom: Alice, Dottie, Irene, Dottie Gunn
at Peggy's Wedding**

**Top: Kenneth, George, Vern
Bottom: Earl, Stan and C.J.**

This old ad from Absorbine Jr. is a good way to learn about "Dudes!"

You maybe never heerd the strains
a lonesome guitar sings.
You maybe never felt them pains
that ridin' sometimes brings.

There's chances you ain't smelt no sage,
nor never caught no trout.
Well, Mister, I'd most purely 'gage
you ain't been here about.

You'll see your steak upon the hoof,
the weaners forked and brand.
Perhaps, you think you'd like to loaf
or be a top cowhand.

And while I'm talkin' you might say
a weaner's what you eat.
Well, so it is — but not that way —
Out here they've got _four_ feet

A rope ain't just a piece of cord
we use to trip a dude.
"To floor" don't mean to use some board.
"To stick" don't mean it's glued.

Mulligan ain't no name o' man.
A bronc is not a cold.
And when a feller mentions _pan_
— that's how they look for gold.

Remuda ain't a new resort
A dogey's not a dog.
Nor punchin ain't a kind o' sport.
A grunter ain't a hog.

Absorbine Jr. ad - Page 2

A cinch is not a thing that's easy.
A longhorn's not to blow.
"Fan" don't mean to make it breezy.
A stage is how you go.

Nor sunfish ain't a thing what swims.
A hump is not a hill.
A wagon tree it don't have limbs.
Nor's pacing a quadrill.

A prairie puss is not so nice
with which to play around.
Two mooses doesn't make them mice.
A "forty" may mean ground.

Nor is a pack for cigarettes.
The elks is not a club.
You can't use cache to make your bets.
Vittles, they're called grub.

Ten gallon ain't a thing to drink.
A bal' face don't mean shaved.
Nor is a gander what you think.
And hardtack don't mean paved.

A butte does not mean pretty girls.
A jamboree won't play.
A prairie oyster don't have pearls.
And sun-up means it's day.

A stud is never what you wear.
And chile is not cool.
Draws is far from underwear.
A jackass ain't a mule.

Absorbine Jr. ad - Page 3

Absorbine Jr. ad - Page 4

Cimarron Guest Ranch
Peekskill, New York
1938 - 1963

Cimarron Ranch

Jim Gunther, Vern and Lu Walter, and Mike Hastings (standing)

Vern and Lu Walter started Cimarron Ranch in 1939. Lu was the guiding force of the ranch - directing all facets. She was the gracious hostess at Cimarron, and it was a resort to be proud of. Every part of it was pristine, but still had the warmth to delight their guests. Lu was a city girl and had never been to a ranch before, but she and Vern made a great team. At Cimarron she kept busy taking care of the reservations, bookkeeping, and overseeing the menus and dining rooms.
A very special guest of the ranch was Loan Walter. Loan was the father of C.J., Verne and Loren. He was a true gentleman. He was well educated, and principal of a school in Detroit, Michigan. After Grandpa's wife passed away, he spent his summers at Cimarron ranch, sitting on the porch and telling stories. No one could believe he was pushing 100 years old.

Excerpts of the Cimarron Brochure:

"You will find Cimarron nestling in a secluded area of Putnam County, New York in a world of its own. Mountains, valleys, lakes and streams that provide a perfect setting for this famous guest ranch, Cimarron. Clean comfortable sleeping accommodations will please you. Food is delicious and abundant. Saddle horses are the greatest, and trails are the finest!

When guests leave this ranch, they feel they are leaving family behind. Most everyone comes back "home."

Riding is the number one sport and activity at Cimarron. Horses are continuously culled and replaced. Riders are grouped by regular, intermediate and beginner sections so that personal help and encouragement can be given to every guest. As all riders agree, there is nothing to compare with the zestful joy of riding, and Cimarron is the place to enjoy it. Because many of our guests are beginners, special care and attention is given to the instruction group. This group progresses under careful leadership, and many "Dudes" join the "experienced riders" before the end of their vacation.

To perpetuate and preserve the flavor of the Old West, a replica of an old western town was built at Cimarron It occupies an area between the main ranch quarters and the stables and rodeo arena, providing a focal point for the lighter side of life. It has a general store for immediate ranch needs; a Last Chance Saloon, typically Western, yet so competently managed, it is a credit to the ranch operation; also a restaurant for a late snack or a hot cup of coffee when the main dining-room is closed; the famous Powder River Hotel for real Western living; and a large dance pavilion."

Above is the artist rendering of
"Westerntown" by Paul Laune
- Below - the dream realized.

Cimarron Ranch Memories

Irene Walter

When we left Canada, Mom sold all her prized possessions and left with just her clothes. Kenneth and Stan stayed with friends in Canada to finish school. Vern and Allan were working in the States, and Peggy was living in Detroit. We stopped in Detroit on the way east, met our relatives and visited with our sister Peggy.

In the spring of 1939, Uncle Verne needed our father at Cimarron, so our Mom, Dad, and our younger siblings left for New York State. I stayed in Detroit until Cimarron Ranch was ready to open. I was needed at the ranch, but hated to leave my new relatives.

I did leave, and hitched a ride from one of the ranch hands who made a trip to Detroit to pick up the ranch's new station wagon.

When we arrived at Cimarron Ranch, I loved the beauty of that valley in Putnam County, New York.

Cimarron Ranch was elegant and beautifully managed. The dining room was sparkling clean and the service was superb. Aunt Lu was a great manager and ran a tight ship. She inspected the furniture wearing white gloves and was a gracious hostess. Each new guest was as smitten with the ranch as I was. Uncle Vern was probably the most handsome man I had ever known. He wore beautifully tailored western clothes, was tall, dark haired, and had a beaming smile.

When I was shown the rest of the ranch, I

Irene Walter

was just awe struck. On the way down to the stable you walked through "Westerntown."

A world famous artist and illustrator named Paul Laune had designed this mock western town and it was built exactly as he meant it to be. The street had a boardwalk. You walked past the dance hall, the cafe, the bar, and the saddle shop before you entered a huge corral where the rodeos were held; then on to the stables where the horses were kept. I had never personally been so close to a horse, but even the smell of the stable was like ambrosia to me. The barns were run by Mike Hastings, a cowboy who had ridden in rodeos for over 30 years before settling in as trail and barn boss at Cimarron.

The ranch had a little cottage on the hill above the main house for our family. Mom would go down to the dining room to help the waitresses and kitchen staff. Then she would take nice hot meals up to the family. We stayed at Cimarron for a very short time until we moved to Cinnabar Ranch. Our father now looked like a movie character. He wore Western clothing; cowboy boots and a Stetson hat that made him look like a hand in the movies. C.J. was a clone of Will Rogers. He would push his hat back off his face, and grin, even when he was speaking.

Cimarron Ranch Memories

Doreen Sloan

My first memory of Cimarron takes me back to when I was nine years old. We were living in Regina, Saskatchewan, Canada. I would sit on my bed with a pamphlet of the Cimarron Guest Ranch. It was full of detailed sketches of the ranch, depicting the four seasons. It was like a dream world to this little girl. I could imagine myself skiing down the hill by the barn. I also wondered how many horses that barn could hold. I had no idea of what a rodeo field was for, and for that matter, tennis courts. Pictures of a beautiful Western Town and a lake down the slope from the main house just took my breath away.

The next year we took off for this new life by Greyhound bus; Mom, Dad, Irene, Earl, George, Maxine and me. My life would never be the same again. At the ranch everyone, even our family, called my mother and father Connie and C.J respectively. Our new home was a lovely little cottage on the hill overlooking the ranch. There were trees all around and we would make trails down to the ranch to pretend we were invading Indians. The ranch buildings were beautiful, made of stone and lumber with much detail. There was a "Western" town that resembled the Old West, with hitching rails for the horses. We loved exploring the many rooms and running up the stairs that took you to the top level where the guest rooms wrapped around the building. In the center of the building you could look down at the dance hall.

We sure loved that little place and that time of my life holds wonderful memories. One adventure I will never forget was a trip we took to New York City to see my brother Allan. He was working for the advertising agency that published the Dude Ranch brochures. I remember looking out of the windows at the cars below and thinking they looked like ants.

That fall Aunt Lu and Uncle Vern took me down to their new winter ranch. It was called the Indian River Ranch in New Smyrna Beach, Florida. I loved it down there. Grandpa Walter insisted we swim every morning in the sulfur pool for our health.

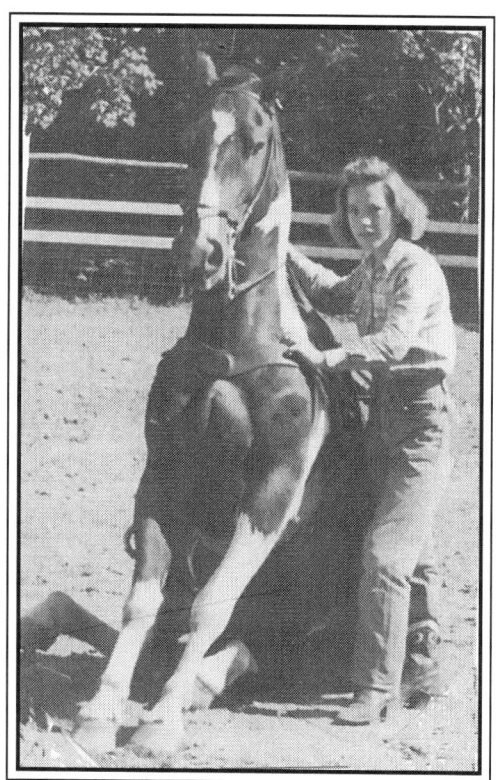

Doreen Walter and Navajo

A young red headed kid and his cousin used to ride over to the stables every day and visit with Mike Hastings and my brother Earl. His name was Red Sloan and he had the cutest southern accent. That is where and how I met my future husband. This Florida Guest Ranch had its own Cabana on the beach. We would take the rides over the causeway and then along the beach. We'd have lunch or supper by the ocean and sometimes ride home by moonlight. What an incredible time!

My brother Allan came down to relieve Uncle Vern and Aunt Lu. My sister Irene became his assistant.

Back at Cimarron, most of the family had jobs. The three youngest children didn't have to work. This gave us plenty of time to ride our horses, walk the trails and visit with Mike Hasting, the old cowboy who ran the barns. It was his job to keep the cowboys in line and coordinate the three rides for the guests. These were beginners, medium and advanced rides. We loved to watch them all get ready.

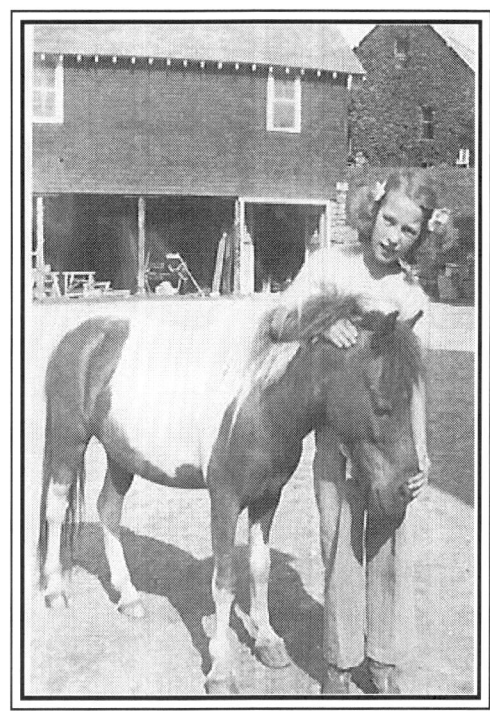
Doreen and Chico

On Sundays, my dad C.J., Uncle Vern, and Mike would put on a great rodeo show. The guests were encouraged to ride in the grand entry carrying many different flags and to ride in the rodeo events if they wanted to. My older brothers learned to do steer riding, calf roping, bulldogging and ride bareback bucking horses. It was just expected that they would ride in all the events, sooner or later.

We weren't at Cimarron long. When my Dad and brother Allan acquired the Cinnabar Ranch, four miles down the road, we all packed up and moved. At that point, all of us kids were old enough to have a job at the ranch. It was fun to be a part of the family business.

George and Doreen Walter

Cimarron's Main House

Cimarron's Dining Room

Horse Corral at Cimarron Ranch

A beautiful view of the Ranch

Artistic Shot of Westerntown

View of Cimarron's Rodeo Corral

Cimarron Ranch
Peekskill, New York
Brochure

Cimarron Ranch Brochure – Front cover

Nestling snugly in a secluded area on Canopus Brook in the rugged hill section of Putnam County, barely 50 miles from New York City, yet in a world of its very own, you will find CIMARRON RANCH. Surrounding mountains, valleys, lakes and streams provide a perfect setting for this famous guest ranch. Clean and comfortable sleeping accommodations will please you. A consistently delicious and abundant table will delight you. As fine a string of saddle horses as you'd want to see or ride, and a sports and entertainment program thoughtfully arranged for you, will, without question, prove the perfect answer to a perfect vacation.

CIMARRON is owner-operated. Lu and Vern Walter and Jim Gunter are your hosts. Vern was born in South Dakota and has lived and breathed dude-ranching most of his life. His years of experience is your assurance of personal attention to every detail. Lu Walter, the boss' wife, is the friend of many thousands who know her cheery smile. To Lu goes much credit for Cimarron's respected reputation, good housekeeping and friendly personality. Jim Gunter, affable works-manager, prides himself (and pleases everyone) on the tidy and well-groomed appearance of the ranch area.

Cimarron Ranch Brochure – Page 1 - 4

Riding is the "Number One" sport and activity at CIMARRON. Horses are continuously culled and replaced. Riders are grouped by REGULAR, INTERMEDIATE AND BEGINNER sections so that personal help and encouragement can be given to every guest. As all riders agree, there is nothing to compare with the zestful joy of riding, and CIMARRON is the place to enjoy it. Because many of our guests are beginners, special care and attention is given to the instruction group. This group progresses under careful leadership, and many join the experienced riders before the end of their vacation.

To perpetuate and preserve the flavor of the Old West, a replica of an old Western Town was built at CIMARRON. It occupies an area between the main ranch quarters and the stables and rodeo arena, providing a focal point for the lighter side of life. It has a general store for immediate ranch needs; a Last Chance Saloon, typically Western, yet so competently managed, it is a credit to the ranch operation; a restaurant, for a late snack or a hot cup of coffee when the main dining-room is closed; the famous Powder River Hotel for real Western living; and a large dance pavilion which is the center of most evening entertainment. Truly, "never a dull moment at CIMARRON."

Cimarron Ranch Brochure – Page 5 and 8

W HILE horseback riding is tops on the list of sports, there are at hand many other ways of having fun at CIMARRON. Friendly sports directors arrange for fun on the archery range, swimming in the spacious pool, fishing the well-stocked trout stream, hiking the rugged mountain trails, target practice on the shooting range, badminton, ping-pong, horse-shoes or soft-ball, moonlight hayrides, weekly picnics and sound movies. There is something for everyone to do every minute, including just plain sitting in the sun.

M IKE HASTINGS, known and loved for many years by the rodeo cowboy, deserves the tribute of having Cimarron's rodeo arena named in his honor, "THE MIKE HASTINGS ARENA." One of the early steer wrestlers, he held the world's championship, in this event, for many years. He is shown above training a Brahma bull to ride. Mike, personally, selects the riding horses for CIMARRON and is in charge of their daily care. He keeps the saddles under constant repair assuring you, and the horse, of having saddles that are both comfortable and safe. Mike leads the parade of guests and contestants that precedes our Sunday rodeos during the summer.

Cimarron Ranch Brochure – Page 9 - 12

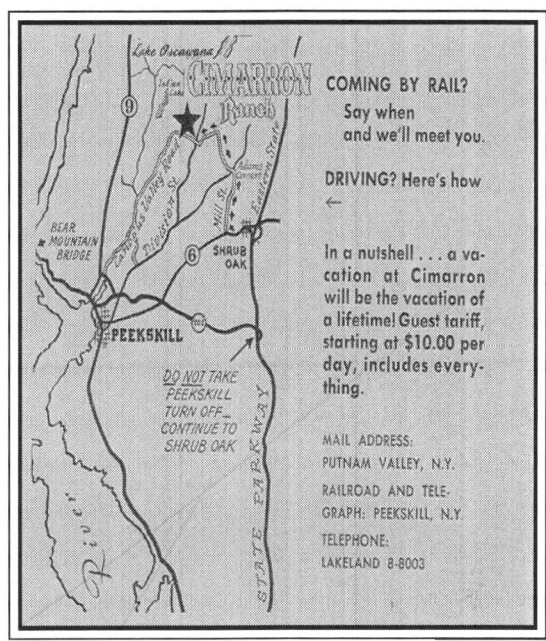

CIMARRON is managed by an adequate staff of competent employees, many of whom, literally, "grew up" with us. They give to CIMARRON that true feeling of homeliness that is so cherished by us and so admired by others. They make you feel "at home," whether it is your first visit or your annual return to the resort where you can be assured of pleasant relaxation, and a happy vacation. Just a tip about clothes . . . dressy clothes are not necessary! Any sports clothes are ideal! Transportation to church is provided! The Sunday morning ride to Mass at GRAYMOOR is a ranch feature!

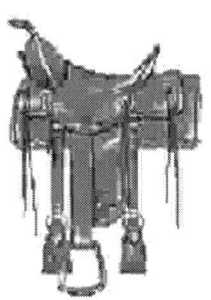

Cimarron Ranch Brochure – Page 13 - 15

A guest waving from the Cimarron and Cinnabar Ranch Stagecoach

Westerntown and Stagecoach

New York Herald Tribune
Sunday, July 13, 1941
Within Site of the Empire State Building

Or Putting the Reverse On Horace Greeley

West of the Canopus

This is no screen set. The picture was taken on the main stem of Cimarron Ranch, in Putnam County just north of the Westchester line, where rootin', shootin' cowgals from Albany and Kew Gardens and hard-bitten clerks from Wall Street go western for relaxation.

**Within Site of the Empire State Building –
New York Herald Tribune - July 13, 1941**

At this Eastern Dude Ranch, which is one of several set up in the metropolitan area by authentic Westerners, real cowboys strum the airs which used to tickle the heart of Will Rogers and Charles M. Russell.

A Man, a Horse and his Girl

The horses are Western Ponies. Many of the cowboys are contestants from the Madison Square Garden rodeos whose high-heeled riding boots have become stuck in the paving of the city streets.

**Within Site of the Empire State Building -
New York Herald Tribune - July 13, 1941**

Saturday Night in Canopus
Guests at the ranch join with the cowboys in shuffling and stamping through the graces of old square dances and reels, with Fifth Avenue slacks and the microphone for the dance caller clashing with the authentic backgrounds.

Men of Dallas in the Hollow
A job of work in the morning sunshine of the Putnam County hills—the boys of the Cimarron ranch picking out a few horses with lariats in the corral.
Photographs by Carroll Van Ark

- 31 -

Irene Walter on Navajo on advertising flyer for Cinnabar Ranch

Maxine and Doreen at Entrance of Cinnabar Ranch

Cinnabar Ranch
Peekskill, New York
1940 - 1946

Birdseye View of Cinnabar Ranch

"The Outside of a horse is good
for the inside of man."

Excerpts from the Cinnabar Ranch Brochure

"Cinnabar Ranch is an approved dude ranch and a charter member in the Eastern Dude Ranch Association. Vernon, Allen and C.J. were some of the earliest members to this organization. Any ranch that was accepted in this organization gives the assurance of an excellent diversified outdoor vacation.

Cinnabar Ranch is one of these new popular and worthwhile types of vacation that will relax you mentally and physically in the healthy tree scented out doors. We feel that our string of western saddle horses is the best, and you can enjoy at least three hours of riding every day

There are always guests at Cinnabar, so never fear of being "alone." Weekends are crowded and a big square dance is the highlight of Saturday evening. Sunday is "Rodeo Day."

Wearing apparel at the ranch is always informal. Bring Levis, or any riding clothes. Wear shirts, sweatshirts, slacks and low-heeled shoes, and you will be in style. Bring a jacket because evenings are cool. If your wardrobe is short of anything, there is a ranch store that carries novelties, boots, Levis, hats, and all you will need.

The "Ranchiest Ranch in the East" is located in the beautiful Sprout Brook section of Putman Valley just four miles north of Peekskill and fifty miles from New York City. It is easily accessible from all main roads leading from New York, Bridgeport, Albany, Boston, and Detroit, and a direct train ride from New York City. Cinnabar is the former Stuyvesant Fish estate composed of tremendous barns, corrals, ample accommodations and recreation facilities. A five-mile private valley through which trails of all description go many miles in each direction encompasses it. The unspoiled beauty of this valley will startle and amaze you. Here far away from subways and elevators, there is a Western Welcome waiting you.

Cinnabar is owned and operated by members of the Walter Family, who were pioneers in offering this ideal vacation. Their greatest pleasure is to provide their guests a real Western Vacation.

On your next vacation come to Cinnabar Ranch where you live as we do in the west, and find miles of exciting mountain and valley land. Land teeming with excellent riding trails that wanders miles and miles right through ranch property. This seclusion of 3000 acres, private lake and ranch loving crowds will assure your full enjoyment of this vacation in a completely carefree manner. Cinnabar is open most of the year. ~

Spring at Cinnabar Ranch . . .

Spring was a time to learn to ride or pick out your horse for the season. Long rides, boating, and dances were also options until the warm weather allowed swimming.

Summer at the Ranch . . .

Summer was a wonderful time at Cinnabar. The large public lake was a popular spot and was equipped with boats, canoes, diving tower, diving board, and a huge float out in the lake. Other activities included picnics, evening hayrides, campfires, square dances, and outdoor movies. Other options included sitting on a deck chair on the lawn, relaxing in your room, or sitting on the wide-open porches.

Catching the big one ...

Ranch Trail Ride

Guests relaxing on the lawn ...

Peggy Walter doing the Virginia Reel

Fall at the Ranch . . .

Stanley Walter and his son joining in the evening's Entertainment

The early fall, with its bright dry sunshine and brisk evenings, was the beckoning call for large numbers of people who appreciated the great outdoors and were able to take their vacations after the summer season had been ushered out by Labor Day. All the various sports at Cinnabar were still available. Guests had excellent facilities for swimming, fishing, boating, golf, and tennis at their disposal, but riding was naturally the main occupation of the day.

Later, about Columbus Day, the leaves were a full riot of changing color and sharply contrasted with the pine trees that encircled the ranch. During this season the numerous activities made days seem too short. A rodeo on Sunday afternoon was the same as in the summer; hot dogs over a campfire with a cowboy singing haunting western tunes-hay rides to some distant spot or a moonlight ride in the brisk air. During the entire year you could be assured of good food and plenty of it, for a satisfied appetite. This is the immediate desire of "dude ranchers" who had been in the open for as little as a first few hours. You'd find yourself with the appetite and we'd supply its demands.

Winter . . .

Winter was the season for those who liked to hear the crisp crunch of snow underfoot, those who liked to skim over lakes and rivers on sharp blades, and those who liked to feel the rush of cool air against their cheeks while riding, skating, skiing or tobogganing. There were always guests at Cinnabar during the week and the weekends were crowded with people who liked to combine winter sports with riding. Special parties were planned for holiday weekends such as Thanksgiving, Christmas, New Year, Lincoln's or Washington's Birthday

The evening entertainments changed with the seasons and mood of the guests-sometimes a movie, roller-skating at the local rink, or bowling. Ordinarily, entertainments such as the Saturday night dance were planned at the ranch.

Winter riding was just as enjoyable as any other season. The horses were all sharp-shod and sure-footed. The same trails were traveled at all times. You could ride both morning and afternoon, if you could find time and all the other sports were available. When snow conditions were right it was a great thrill to get behind a horse on skis with a reliable partner.

Montana Guest Cottage

Doreen, Dottie and Maxine Walter

California Guest Rooms

Ranch Activities

Alyce Walter, Ivy Goodale, Charlotte Walter, C.J. Walter, Doreen Walter, and Allan Walter

The first thing that amazed our guests was the friendly atmosphere. Everyone was called by their first name, and the informal dining style, no assigned seats, made it impossible to be a loner, even if you wanted to be. You would meet new guests every meal and it was a real family atmosphere. Our cook planned simple, tasty food, and no one left the table hungry. When the dinner bell rang, the hot food, in large bowls, would be put on the tables family style. The waitresses refilled these bowls as often as needed, but if you were late, you might get there when desert was being served. We think this may be why the informal get-togethers before dinner on Montana's front porch (right near the dining room!) was a nightly ritual and very handy when the dinner bell rang. The help ate at the same time; their table was right next to the guest dining area. All the hands and our family that ate at the helps table would laugh and have a great time. This made the atmosphere friendlier and more personable, loosening up the feeling of being in a new place for the guests.

Daily Rides

This was the main activity at the ranch. Three different groups of riders went out every morning and afternoon. There was a fast ride for experienced riders. These folks were given the more spirited horses and taken on a longer ride, usually over to our sister ranch Cimarron. The intermediate ride was for folks who had ridden before, but wanted to slowly get used to the activity again. We had miles of beautiful trails. Most went through the meadows where the horses grazed at night, and around the lake, but there were several long stretches where an easy lope was enjoyed. This ride usually ended up at Cimarron Ranch also. The slow ride was the choice for first-time guests. These horses were well trained and were not too spirited. This ride rambled over the many acres of the ranch property. Most riders would ask for the same horse each ride. The hands that looked after the horses were very capable, caring and handsome fellows. The guests were their most important job and these Levi clad, western-hat wearing guys were charmers.

Another amazing experience for many city folks happened every evening when all the horses on the ranch were turned loose. One of the hands would lead them out, with couple of hands bring up the rear. If you were invited along, this was something you would never forget. The horses were herded down the road, then turned left over a stream. It was a slow process because many of the horses would stop to drink. Then the horses were herded left again into the great pastures that the ranch owned. When they were all pastured, the herders would head home, making sure all gates were secured. This was a very relaxing way to end the day.

s go! Ride leaving corral at Cinnabar Ranch, Peekskill, N. Y. " The Ranchiest Ranch in the East "

Swimming and Boating

The very impressive man-made lake at Cinnabar was great for cooling off after a long day of riding. The dandy beach was great for building a campfire in the evenings. The ranch had canoes and rowboats and a great raft with a diving board, far enough out for a nice swim, and a great place to relax and sunbathe. The beach wasn't closed down at night, so boating was a wonderful moonlight activity. There was a little island that could be explored, giving you a feeling of being Robinson Caruso. At the end of the lake was a man-made dam and the water flowing over it to the streams below had a magical sound.

Square Dances

Saturday night was special. All the help wore their best tailor-made clothes. Some of these outfits were just beautiful. We had a western band and if you thought you couldn't do these dances, your mind was changed. You could learn to do the Square Dance, the Polka, or the Schottische; a round dance similar to the Polka, but slower. These affairs were well attended and no one was happy when the band went home. Western music has a special charm, and there was usually a singing cowboy who would lead a songfest during intermission. C.J. always asked the band to play his favorite songs; "Oh Susanna," "Red Wing," and "On Top of Ole Smokey." How we miss his contagious attitude, and his true love of people.

Initiations

Monday night was initiation night. The guests would be called to the lower level of the main hall. They would all gather in a circle and be introduced. C.J. would pretend he could hypnotize a person. They would choose a candidate and she or he would be taken out of the hall. The guests would decide what they would want her to act out. He would send a person back to bring the candidate out and of course he would tell her what the deal was. There was always a lot of amazement and everyone was such a good sport and a lot of fun.

This was a relaxing evening and of course refreshments were served. This was a good icebreaker for new guests. My dad and Stan made this evening special. My mother's little store was at the end of the room, and this was a time when all the hard working family and crew could really relax and get to know our guests better. The ranch help didn't have regular hours and entertaining the guests was just part of the job.
C.J. called it Color! And it was.

Initiation Night

Picnic Rides and Pack Trips

Weekly picnics were fun. A guitar-picking cowboy was always there and our cook packed wonderful, abundant food and everyone would be really tired after the whole day out in the countryside. Most of these rides were lengthy, some going to Greymoor Monastery, a very quaint and famous place. Overnights were planned if the guests at the time were hardy or interested enough.

Outdoor activities before, after and during trail rides

Getting ready for the hayride

Hay Rides

Thursday was Hay Ride night. A wagon filled with fresh smelling hay, pulled by a team of horses, left the stables packed full of Cinnabar's guests. It would travel the road between Cinnabar and Cimarron, approximately a four-mile ride. Every old song in the book would be sung and all had a great time. This night was special because the guests were invited to Cimarron's mid week dance. After the dance, happy, tired guests would be taken back to Cinnabar in the wagon. What a great evening!

Wagon load of guests

The Original Fish Farm

The Stagecoach leading the Trail Ride

CINNABAR DUDE RANCH

PEEKSKILL, N.Y.

Cinnabar Ranch is the former Stuyvesant Fish Estate, just fifty miles from New York in beautiful Putnam Valley. The ranch has two private lakes and 1000 acres of grazing land and riding trails.

MEMBER OF EASTERN DUDE RANCH ASSOCIATION

A Little Doggie Strays From the Herd—Why Don't You?

Introduction to a New Phase of Dude Ranch History

As never before, folks in all walks of life are going to share a desire to get away from the pressure of high speed work during our war years. Men going into the service, on furlough or returning from oversea's duty have the urge to spend several weeks of diversified outdoor enjoyment before leaving for camp. Girls will find themselves looking at resort folders though they have never taken the opportunity to vacation in the past.

And—dude ranching is the one new, popular and worthwhile type vacation, for it will relax you mentally and physically in the healthy, tree-scented outdoors.

CINNABAR finds a place for itself in this picture by providing the finest in this particular type of outdoor life enjoyment. The following pages will tell (and we hope, convince) you about Cinnabar.

3

C. J. WALTER with four of his sons now serving Uncle Sam

CINNABAR
The Ranchiest Ranch in the East

Cinnabar is located in the beautiful Sprout Brook section of Putnam Valley just 4 miles north of Peekskill and 50 miles from metropolitan New York. It is easily accessible from all main roads and railroads leading from New York, Bridgeport, New Haven, Boston, Albany, Detroit, Cleveland and Pittsburgh.

Cinnabar is the former Stuyvesant Fish estate composed of tremendous barns, corrals, ample accommodations and

4

- 48 -

You'll Find Real Western Friendliness Here

recreation facilities. It is encompassed by a 5-mile private valley through which trails of all description lead many miles in all directions. The un-spoiled beauty of this valley and adjoining country will startle and amaze.

Here, far away from subways and elevators there is a western welcome awaiting you. We know you will have a good time at Cinnabar as we always do, and as do all who come back here year after year.

Cinnabar is owned and operated by members of the Walter family who have been in the Eastern Dude Ranch business for many years and their greatest pleasure is derived from providing their guests with a real western vacation. They cordially invite you to visit the ranch any time you happen to be in the neighborhood.

Relaxing before the dinner bell rings

Planning a Vacation? Cinnabar is the Answer

SPRING
In the spring cowboy and cowgirl thoughts lightly turn to love and preparations for a busy summer season. For some people spring is by far the most enjoyable season of the year for general sports and especially riding.

Upon his arrival at Cinnabar each person may try various horses until one that is entirely suitable is acquired. The corral boss will then try to hold this horse for you each day. The finest of reliable western horses are kept at Cinnabar. Horses for beginners as well as advanced riders are at hand and instruction is free.

During the spring months a person is entitled to ride both morning and afternoon for as long as one desires. Swimming, boating and other sports are available as the season progresses.

There are always guests at Cinnabar so one need not hesitate for fear of being "all alone." Weekends are always crowded and a big square dance is the feature of Saturday night to the tunes of a real square dance orchestra, and our own rodeo on Sunday afternoons.

Wearing apparel of the ranch is always informal. Bring along your regular riding clothes as well as slacks, sweaters, low heeled shoes and a leather jacket, for the evenings are always cool. If your wardrobe is short in any particular we can probably supply it from the ranch store which carries novelties, boots, levis, hats and neckerchiefs.

7

- 49 -

A Home on the Range for You

SUMMER
The success of Cinnabar is natural for it has all the requisites to make dude ranching the most popular and acceptable type vacation, and they are namely, good food, good horses, good accommodations and an abundance of western personality.

New additions to our buildings have added a number of de luxe accommodations. Your requests for private, double or twin rooms will always be met by the addition of these rooms. These rooms as well as the other accommodations are equipped with the finest of beddings and inner spring mattresses.

Our large private lake is one of the most popular spots of the ranch during this season and is well equipped with boats, canoes, diving tower, diving board and a huge float out in the lake. A quick dip before lunch or dinner is especially appreciated.

All day picnics, evening hay rides, camp fire initiations, Saturday night square dances and outdoor movies on Sunday evenings are a few of the extra features at Cinnabar during the summer season.

You can rest—the freedom of ranch life will fit your restful mood perfectly. You can relax in your own comfortable room or in the main ranch house lounge rooms and open porches. You can sink into a deck chair on the sunny lawn or on the beach forgetting about the rushing traffic, crowded subways and smoke of the city.

10

- 50 -

The Walter Family Own and Direct Cinnabar

WINTER is the season for those who like to hear the crisp crunch of snow underfoot, those who like to skim over lakes and rivers on sharp blades and those who like to feel the rush of cool air against their cheeks riding, skating, skiing or tobogganning.

There are guests at Cinnabar during the week and the weekends are always crowded with people who like to combine winter sports with riding. Special parties are planned for weekends such as Christmas, New Year, Lincoln's or Washington's Birthday.

The evening entertainments change with the seasons and mood of the guests. Sometimes a movie, roller skating at the local rink or bowling. Ordinarily entertainments such as the Saturday night dance are planned at the ranch and these are a few of the extra features that may be enjoyed while at the ranch.

Winter riding is just as enjoyable as any other season. The horses are all sharp-shod and sure footed. The same trails are travelled at all times and you may ride both morning and afternoon if you can find time for the other sports that are available. When snow conditions are right it is a great thrill to get behind a horse on skis with a reliable partner to pull you along. There's nothing in the world like it.

You'll always find a real western atmosphere at Cinnabar, your home on the range among congenial companions, and you'll find every trail full of thrills and romance.

Nature Cures All Ills

FALL The early fall with its bright dry sunshine and brisk evenings is the beckoning call for great numbers of people who appreciate the great outdoors and are able to take their vacations after the summer season has been ushered out by Labor Day. All the various sports at Cinnabar are still available. Guests have excellent facilities for swimming, fishing, boating, golf and tennis at their disposal, but riding is naturally the main occupation of the day. (All free to guests except golf).

Later, about Columbus Day, the leaves are a full riot of changing color and sharply contrast themselves with the pine trees which encircle the ranch. During this season the numerous activities make days seem too short. A rodeo Sunday afternoon the same as in the summer—hot dogs over a campfire with a cowboy singing haunting western tunes—hay rides to some distant spot—a moonlight ride in the brisk air.

During the entire year you can be assured of good food and plenty of it for a satisfied appetite is the immediate desire of dude ranchers who have been in the open for as little as the first few hours. You'll find yourself with the appetite and we'll supply its demands.

On your fall vacation come to Cinnabar Ranch where you live as we do in the west, and find miles of exciting mountain and valley land. Land teeming with excellent riding trails that wander miles and miles right on ranch property. This seclusion of 3000 private acres, private lake and ranch loving crowds will assure your full enjoyment of this vacation in a completely carefree manner.

14

There's tonic in the smell of green pine and saddle leather

Land of the Saddle, Rope and Spur

Transportation
By train — New York Central trains leave Grand Central Station regularly and the ranch station wagon will meet you in Peekskill on certain specified trains. Railroad fare from New York is $1.08. By car — from New York — Henry Hudson Parkway to Hawthorne Circle, continue on Bronx River Parkway Extension to Peekskill, N. Y. From the Parkway turn right through Rock-Cut near Peekskill. Take first right turn after the Rock-Cut.

Reservations
Our clientele has been restricted to 75 this year to enable us to give you the utmost in comfort and congeniality. You will find our guests have been carefully selected and restricted to those who have a natural love for good horses and a genuine western atmosphere and hospitality. You will not be disappointed in their company. A $10.00 deposit is required on each reservation before it is made definite. This deposit is applied to your bill. However, if a cancellation must be made your deposit will be returned if we are notified in advance. If you wish further information or want to make a reservation write directly or call Cinnabar Ranch, Peekskill, N. Y., 402.

Sports
Horseback riding, bicycle riding, archery, ping pong, dancing, badminton, horseshoes, rifle range, and canoeing, boating and swimming on our private lake. We also have hayrides, initiations, moonlight rides, picture shows and a rodeo each Sunday. There is always something doing.

Accommodations
New accommodations this year will have running hot and cold water in the building "California."

19

A Quick Recap of Activities at Cinnabar

Riding
During the summer there will be two riding periods each day from two to three hours duration each. The weekly rate includes one riding period each day. Weekend rates include one riding period Saturday and a ride Sunday. Extra rides may be arranged at any time for $3.00 per extra session. Persons who go to church Sunday morning may ride Sunday afternoon. Cinnabar can boast of having the finest string of western saddle horses in the east — as every ride is thoroughly enjoyed.

Private Horses... are boarded at the ranch for our guests, and the ranch has for sale at all times, outstanding saddle horses and equipment.

Rodeo
A typical western rodeo is a Sunday afternoon feature. It is a pleasure to watch our guests participating in the games and contests. Cinnabar has a large herd of rodeo stock so this event is looked forward to by our ranch hands as well as the guests.

Clothing
Riding clothes you may have will suffice at the ranch and you may purchase levis, shirts and neckerchiefs at the ranch store. Slacks are very suitable evening wear and be sure to bring along sweaters and a leather jacket. Evenings are quite cool even during the summer months.

Church
Catholic and Protestant churches are within short distance of the ranch. Guests without cars are taken to church in the ranch station wagon.

18

This Year Let's Go Western

- 53 -

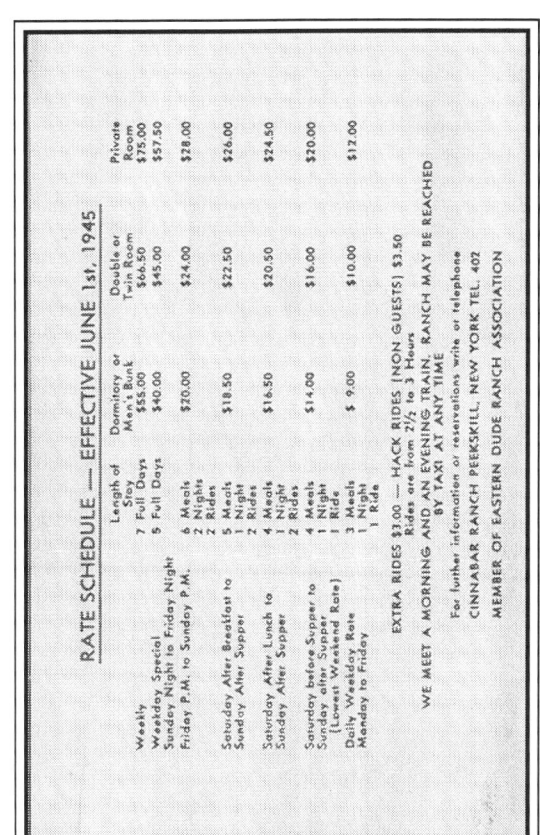

Allan Walter and Navajo
Riding along the Lake at Cinnabar

This lake was a man-made lake
Added to the farm by Stuyvesant Fish

Young George's barn    Cinnabar Ranch Sign

Cinnabar Barn Yard

Top: Tom and Irene Brown, Doreen Walter, Dottie Cooper, C.J.,
Maxine Walter, Marge and Bill Stanfield
Bottom: Earl Walter, Harry Tompkins, a guest's child, Joe Breckenridge,
George Stump, George Walter

Taking the horses out to pasture

Cimarron: Top Row: Mike, George, Eddie, Cliff, Doc, Bob, Billy, Eddie, and Bill
Bottom Row: Hub, Jonny, Rip, Harry, Vern, Skinner, Mike, Johnny, Frank, Jim and George

The stone walls in front of "California"

Harry Tompkins

Vern, Loan, and C.J. Walter
Welcome all to Rodeo

Rodeos

Red Sloan Calf Roping

- 58 -

Rodeos

When C.J. started the rodeos at Cinnabar, he told his children they would all ride and perform for the first time. Rodeo events included saddle broncos, bareback riding, and bull riding. Doreen really felt special because she had her own act, starting with riding her pony, "Chico," and then going on to trick riding. I guess there must have been some natural talent there as we all rode, and enjoyed it. Irene was quite a seamstress and presented C.J. with colored matching satin shirts for the Quadrille team, a different color for each pair of riders. He sure was proud of the effect.

We had many very talented hands come up from Staten Island with their horses that would rodeo and trick ride, or help in any way. C.J. loved the added "color." These folks would sit down with the help when the dinner bell rang and it was great visiting with them. These talented people loved our ranch and they became good friends. Many of our novices went on to rodeo for a living. Both Cinnabar and Cimarron sponsored many of them in Madison Square Garden, which was one of the best rodeos on the rodeo circuit.

Mike Hastings had been a world champion bulldogger for many years and was pleased to be back in the arena again. Harry Tompkins, another world champion rodeo rider, started his career riding at the ranches. Red Sloan and Earl Walter also went on to the "Garden" to compete in the rodeos.

George Walter

Charlotte Walter leading the Rodeo Parade

Rodeo Contests

Wild Horse Race - This race is a group of 8 wild range horses and 8 foolhardy men who try to race them to a finish line. The horses are usually the wildest horses they can find and special prizes were given for the rider of the "worst" horse. A three man team would be needed to get the rider on the horse - then spurs and courage would be needed to guide the horse to the finish line.

Wild Bull Riding - This is considered to be the most dangerous event of the rodeo. Brahma bulls, the ride of choice, are wild and vicious. They are quick and will turn and gore their rider if he happens to fall. Because of the danger and injuries, this is a popular event. The rider must have one hand free at all times and the other holding a loose rope without knots or hitches. The rider must stay on eight seconds before falling or dismounting. Rodeo clowns come in and risk their lives to distract the bulls away from their riders.

Wild Steer Wrestling - This event is also called "bulldogging," and the cowboy rides his fast, highly trained horse up to the bull, then leaps to the head of the bull. Then it is a hand-to-horn battle, with the bull weighing at least four times more than his opponent. Another cowboy called a "hazer" rides next to the bull to keep his course as straight as possible. This event started as an exhibition stunt - and then progressed into a rodeo event. Mike Hastings, trail boss at Cimarron and Cinnabar ranches, held the record in 1916 of 12 seconds.

Bareback Bronco Riding - This is a very dangerous event that stems from the traditional battle between man and beast in frontier days, when horses belonged to the person that could catch and ride them. The horse does not wear saddle or bridle. There is a surcingle around the withers, a form of strap with a handle on top. The rider must have one hand free at all times, and be "scratching" at all times. This means the cowboy must be spurring the horse in the shoulders throughout the ride to make him very ornery. The ride lasts ten seconds and then pickup men ride out and distract the bronco while they pick up the rider.

Wild Calf Roping - Calf roping is a team sport of the west. The horse and his training is as important as the roper in this contest. The cowboy ropes the calf, and then the horse holds the rope taut without tugging on it or dragging the calf more than three feet, while the cowboy throws the calf by hand and ties three feet together. The roper then signals "Time" to the judges, and they ride over to judge his performance, horse, and tie.

Saddle Bronc Riding - This is the most "stylish" and colorful event of the rodeo. The rider has a saddle and one rein, but an artistic performance is demanded by the judges. The rider must be scratching as in the bareback event, and of course, stay on without violating the rules. These rules include failure to scratch with their spurs, changing hands on the reins, wrapping the rein around their hand, losing the rein, pulling on the horses head, hitting the horse with hat or hand, or "pulling leather," or holding or grabbing the saddle in any way.

Walter Rodeo Pictures

Doreen Walter doing the Hippodrome Stand

Doreen Walter

Doreen, Allan, and Charlotte Walter

Doreen Barrel Racing

Doreen doing the Russian Drag

Doreen Practicing

Doreen Practicing with a cast on her leg

Rodeos – Real Crowd Pleasers at the Ranches

Earl Walter

Earl Walter riding "Hell-O-Fire" at Cinnabar Ranch

Earl

Earl getting ready

Earl Walter Calf Roping

Earl Walter "Bulldogging"

- 65 -

George Walter

Earl and George Walter leading the rodeo parade

George Walter on a "Bronc"

George Walter

George in the Ring

C.J. and Maxine and Victory

Maxine riding the Bull

Maxine Walter

C.J. Snapping a picture of Maxine coming off a bull

Maxine Walter Barrel Racing

Maxine in the Ring

Rodeo Pictures

Red Sloan

Cowboy and Indian Skit

Dottie Walter

A rodeo performer jumping his horse over a car

Bill Schwerd Roman Riding

Cinnabar Rodeo

**Lu Walter on Silver at the
Cimarron Rodeo**

**Bill Schwerd performing his American Flag Trick
At the Rodeo**

One of the Ranch Hands, Finnerty, riding "TNT"

Transferring from One Horse to Another

Madison Square Garden Rodeo 1943

1943: The Walter family and guests at Madison Square Garden rodeo

Yearly Rodeo Party

Every year, when the rodeo was in New York City, we would plan our "Rodeo Party." Invitations were sent to all the guests and ranch hands. Reservations were made at the Belvedere Hotel, just across the street from Madison Square Garden. We made arrangements for a cocktail hour and dinner. Guests like Roy Rogers, Gene Autry, and rodeo contestants would come over to meet our friends. A western band was hired for a square dance after the dinner. It was quite a gala affair and very well attended.

Bottom: Herman Fredericks, Irene and Tom Brown, Gerald and Inez Roberts, Ken Roberts and his wife, Harry Tompkins
Top: Publicity agents, Dixie (Roy's first wife) and Roy Rogers, C.J. Walter, Fog Horn Clancy

CINNABAR
Dude Ranch News

OCTOBER, 1942 — PEEKSKILL, N. Y. — Vol. 2, No. 2

Cinnabar's Annual Rodeo Party-Reunion-Dance to be held October 14th

Earl Walter to Compete for Cinnabar Ranch at the Rodeo

This year's Cinnabar Rodeo Party will have as an innovation the prospect of seeing one of our home-bred (Peekskill) cowboys competing for the Ranch against the best talent in the world. He is Earl Walter, almost 18 years old, and as rough and tough as they come. Earl has been riding bucking horses for the past two years and has made rapid enough strides to justify our nomination of him to compete for Cinnabar Ranch.

Earl received his first taste of rodeo life while being associated with the celebrated Mike Hastings, world famous bronc rider and one time bulldogging champion of the world. Since that time Earl has been riding the toughest broncs he can find and has acquitted himself in such a manner as to make his nomination to represent Cinnabar Ranch unanimous.

Make your reservations for this Annual Cinnabar Rodeo Party as soon as possible, either through our New York Office at 155 East 42nd Street, or directly at the Ranch, at Peekskill, New York. The reunion will be held this year at the Hotel Belvedere for cocktails and dinner. Later to Madison Square Garden, where the best seats available have been secured, then later to the Belvedere for one of our famous get-togethers and dances.

All ranch hands and guests will be in attendance in their regular ranch clothes. There will be rooms provided where folks in the City will have the opportunity to change into ranch clothes before the party begins.

This is the one opportunity that the guests of this year and past years have an opportunity of meeting and greeting each other and to really enjoy themselves in the real western atmosphere of the Rodeo.

It is a good suggestion to send your reservations and money order for this party just as soon as possible. There are a limited number of seats available at the Garden and the first reservations in will be the first ones served. On the back page of the NEWS you will find full details where to send your reservations and the price per person.

Earl Walter riding "TNT" at one of Cinnabar's Sunday Rodeos, in preparation for his entrance to Garden competition. Harry Kielly waits to pick him off.

Cinnabar Dude Ranch News

Gracie Morris fondles Pearl while her pure white colt looks on jealously

PRIVATE HORSES AT RANCH INCREASING IN POPULARITY

During the early spring and summer, incidentally the most successful season in our history, the number of privately owned horses sold and boarded at the Ranch has increased tremendously. The number of persons who are willing to pay for the privilege of having the exclusive use of some favorite horse has also been astonishing.

During the early spring our wily horse trader bought the finest string of western ponies he could find and in turn sold to the most suitable persons the most suitable horses. Cinnabar's horse trader is the personable C. J. Walter, who numbers among his most satisfied horse owners such folk as Babs McAllister, who now owns Lady; Pat Coleman, who decided to own Wascana; Dorothy Tranter, now owner of the very well broke horse, Nova; Dr. Frank Fiero, the proud owner of a beautiful palomino named Pal; Al and Helen Brown, who purchased Smokey and Thunder; Chris Wilson is the proud owner of a big buckskin, Powder River, King, and Victory another Palomino purchased by Percey Rhoades; Ruth Merritt, the new owner of Dakota Red.

In addition to horses purchased at the Ranch, Merve Stratton made a flying trip to Cleveland to purchase a beautiful full Morgan horse; Ed Drews, now in the Navy, sold his horse, Chief, to Bill Merritt and Tina Sire, who lives at the Ranch, owned Jimmie.

Persons who board their horses at the Ranch receive a two dollar credit for each day they are at the Ranch and they have the privilege of riding the horse at any time they desire.

Many Cinnabar Boys and Guests Now in the Armed Forces
Each will receive 10% Discount anytime while at Ranch

The other evening while passing the door of the Stage Door Canteen in New York, the thought flashed through my mind of how many of our former guests and boys who worked at the Ranch are now in an intensive training program and the number who are already overseas.

In addition to the many whom we cannot recall, the following have been guests of the Ranch, and some, boys who have worked there: Blackie Miozza is at Camp Pickett, in Virginia, awaiting transfer to his regular post; Art Pritchard is in a hospital in Palm Springs, California; Bob Lehmann, who trained at Fort Bragg and Fort Sill, is now a 2nd Lieutenant in heavy artillery and is now overseas. The following boys are in the armed forces, but at the present time we do not know their correct rank, place they are stationed or branch of service, but anyone desiring such information may drop a line to the Ranch and we will do everything we can to give the proper data. There are probably many more whom we will not list, but it is only through our lack of knowledge of their induction or enlistment, that they are omitted. The following we know for certain, are doing their share for America: Al Birra, John Golden, Sam Pastorfield, Lem Leavitt, Jack Ahearn, Ed Drews, Fred Reid, Ray Johnson, John Crone, Lew Conaroe, Hank Zelner, Charles Hoffman, Art Beyer, Harold Shaw, Hannes Koops, Hal Reidinger, Jimmie Eichler, Ed May Ed Smythe, Chick Kusmich, Bob Wood, Ernie Clark, Joe Matesysak, Fred Haas, Ned Bryant, John Canning, Doc Ross, John DiGaetano and Pete Bodolaty. Bill Teel, a cowboy from the Ranch, has been in the service for the past year.

It would please us very much if the folks receiving this pamphlet would advise us of any names that might be missing and also forward or ask us to forward a copy of the News to any of the boys mentioned above.

One of the Big Events during our Rodeo season was the first ride made by Maxine Walter on a steer. Stan and C. J. Walter grinning in the background as she makes a good ride.

Cinnabar Dude Ranch News

On the Fire

Did you happen to notice the write-up given the Ranch in the September 5th issue of Liberty or the one in the October issue of Spot Magazine? . . . Three very well known models, Pat Ogden, Grace Morris and Pat Morris posed for hundreds of pictures—don't let anyone tell you modeling is as glamorous as it looks . . . The Ranch now boasts three pure white animals—Pearl White and her colt Silver Dawn, and Carlo, a big shepherd dog. A picture of the three is very striking . . . Terry Thierolf, our very good Philadelphia guest, did work very hard for Cinnabar this summer, also Anne McAlpine, who is from Kew Gardens . . . Two of our favorite cowgirls are Betty & Glenna Smith from just outside Boston, who can make a horse do anything, including the difficult art of trick riding . . . Vern Walter came east early in June to await induction into the Army—he has taken care of the Ranch store and now is one of the cowboys since Blackie went into the Army . . . Fall will soon be upon us and is always the time of year guests who prefer riding come to Cinnabar. It is rumored Bobby Ritter and Al Birza are engaged and will soon be married . . . To remind you we sell Levis and Shirts in our store, reminds us we have had a very good quota of men this summer . . . Stan Walter may be in the Army soon . . . The leaves are taking on their first autumn hues and will be in full color about the middle of October . . . The new accommodations in California have proved well worth while . . . Cowboys at the Ranch get a great kick out of Herman Fredericks' music machine . . . Thanks to Joe Semescze for his aid during one of our rare rainy Sundays, and the very well planned get-together he arranged for September 23rd in New York . . . Kindly forgive me for not mentioning certain events which I know have taken place in the past eight months . . . Drop us a line and I will do better next time . . .

—ALLAN.

I've Got Spurs That—But Romances and Marriages Seem to Boom at Cinnabar

A lot of Ranch romances have been witnessed by us in the past seven years but this is the first year we have had such an epidemic of marriages in which Ranch folks were participants. At least six marriages have been the results of meetings at Cinnabar Ranch.

Early this spring Anne Van Kleeck was married to Ned Bryant while he was on leave from the Navy and later in the summer her sister Joan was married to a western boy whose name we cannot recall at the moment. Soon after returning from Fort Sill, Oklahoma Bob Lehman took Jean Ellis for his bride. Dickie Schaeffer from Baltimore and John Canning of New Jersey (now in the army), were married early this summer. Peggie Edwards and Bill Marshall were married early this spring. After many months of guessing on the part of guests, Charlotte Schaaf and Allan Walter were married early in June, and just a few weeks ago Irene Walter and Tom Brown tied the knot. Tom will be entering the Naval Air Corps in a month or so, as he enlisted two months ago.

From our observations each one of these ropings have been of the most successful sort and our hopes are for the very best in the future.

Huge Rodeo Held at Cinnabar for Local Boys in the Armed Services

One of the most successful rodeos in the life of Eastern Dude Ranches was held at Cinnabar Ranch on September 30th, under the auspices of the Peekskill Service Men's Auxiliary. The Ranches Cinnabar and Cimarron along with the Richmond County Sheriff's Posse (Staten Island) and the Hudson County (New Jersey), combined their resources and talent to make it an outstanding event. The sale of tickets and donations grossed more than three times the amount anticipated by the committee.

Announcements and commentary were very well handled by Frank Steinrock of the Staten Island Sheriff's Posse and Vern Walter. Further information on the events below are pictured on the other pages.

Tom Brown who will shortly be in the Navy Air Corps—and in this case is flying very low as our buckingest steer, "Big Red" cuts loose and is determined to get rid of his excess baggage.

CINNABAR RANCH
PEEKSKILL, N. Y.

4 *Cinnabar Dude Ranch News*

MAKE YOUR RESERVATIONS FOR

Cinnabar's Annual Rodeo
ROUND-UP PARTY

Hotel Belvedere (Opposite Madison Square Garden)   Wednesday, Oct. 14, 1942

PROGRAM

3:00 P.M. to 6:30 P.M.
Receive tickets and souvenirs at the Hotel Belvedere and meet your friends from the Ranch.

6:30 P.M.
Dinner in the main Ballroom of the Hotel Belvedere.

8:00 P.M.
To Madison Square Garden for the thrilling Rodeo.

11:30 P.M.
To the basement to see all the trick horses and bucking stock, then back to the Hotel Belvedere for cocktails and dancing.

The Entire Evening with all Expenses Included is Only $7.50

Send your money order or check as soon as possible to:

CINNABAR RANCH
PEEKSKILL, N. Y.
or take it to our N. Y. office
155 EAST 42ND STREET
Telephone, MUrray Hill 4-2023

Irene Walter rests during her ride.

★ Write to Irene immediately about reservations and seating arrangements

The War Years

This was a tough time for all our families. All of our brothers were in the service, as well as Bill Schwerd, Joe Ferrante and Tom Brown, Irene's husband. Vern served in the Air Force, a mechanic for the planes in Italy. Allan and Stanley served in the US Army. Both men were in the thick of all the war activities in Europe. Kenneth was in the US Army, served in the Aleutians. Bill Schwerd served and was injured in the US Army. Tom Brown was in the Navy and Coast Guard, working with horses and dogs for the beach patrol. The ladies of the family worked hard to stay in the ranch business. The in-laws, Charlotte and Alyce Walter and Milly Prichard were just part of the family. We were up to the challenge. This was a rough time for all of America's families. One year we gathered a huge bunch of Pine bows and sat around one of the large tables in the dining room making wreaths. We were determined to have some Christmas cheer. We listened to Christmas carols and made wreaths to put on every building at the ranch. I don't know who saw the fire first, but the living quarters down by George's barn was on fire. The Peekskill fire company responded very fast, but the living quarters of Connie and C.J. Walter, Alyce and Stan Walter, Artie and Milly Prichard and Earl, George and all the ranch hands were destroyed. When the fire was extinguished, the ladies went back to the dining room and finished the wreaths but without the music and Christmas cheer.

**Stanley, Alyce, Earl, Irene, and Blackie Miozzi
The "Paul Revere" Posse during World War II**

Top Left: In case you want to know, this is the easy way (?) to transfer from a horse to a steer. **Top Right**: Lesson in poise by a trick-horse rider. **Below**: View of the Cinnabar arena as it appeared during the grand opening of the rodeo Sunday afternoon. Part of the crowd of 2000 persons is in the left front lawn on the hillside above the corral.
Star Photos

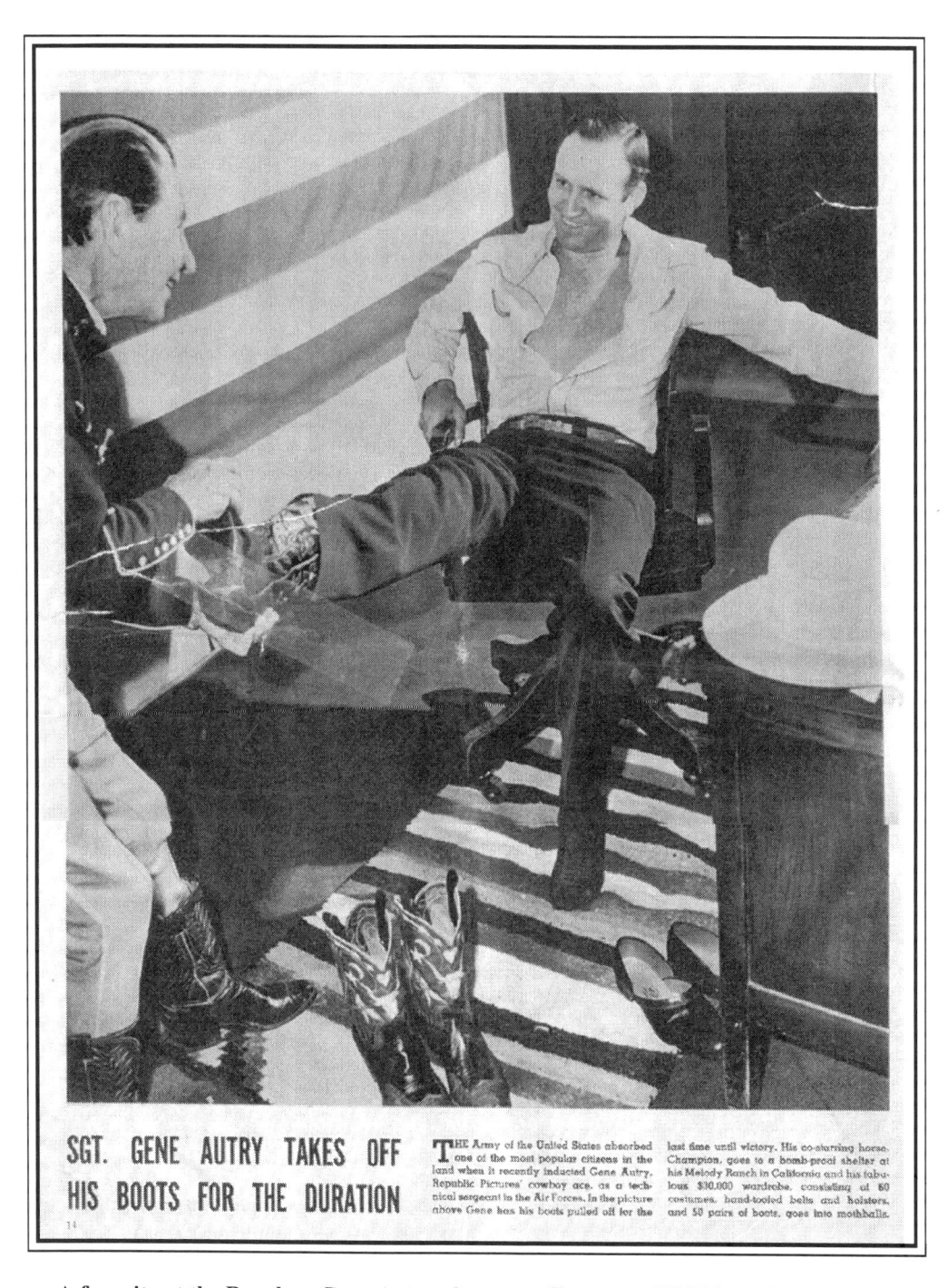

SGT. GENE AUTRY TAKES OFF HIS BOOTS FOR THE DURATION

THE Army of the United States absorbed one of the most popular citizens in the land when it recently inducted Gene Autry, Republic Pictures' cowboy ace, as a technical sergeant in the Air Forces. In the picture above Gene has his boots pulled off for the last time until victory. His co-starring horse, Champion, goes to a bomb-proof shelter at his Melody Ranch in California and his fabulous $30,000 wardrobe, consisting of 50 costumes, hand-tooled belts and holsters, and 50 pairs of boots, goes into mothballs.

A favorite at the Ranches, Gene Autry also goes off to war – PM Magazine, Oct 1941

CINNABAR RANCH
Peekskill, New York

CINNABAR
DUDE RANCH NEWS

1943   Peekskill, New York   Vol. III, No. 1

Cinnabar Enjoys Big Ranch Seasons Despite Manpower Drain of War

The tremendous number of men who have left for duty with the Army, Navy, Marines, and air forces would seem to preclude the possibility of many men being guests of eastern dude ranches. This has not been the case for men on furloughs have found their greatest enjoyment and relaxation in the atmosphere created by the friendliness of dude ranch guests and management.

The strain of long hours and long weeks of work in war plants have also contributed their share of men who often have very little time to enjoy themselves in the open. The government has advised such vacations are to be encouraged and the resultant increased production has justified their view.

For full enjoyment of good horses, riding country unsurpassed, good food and accommodations, a large lake with boating, fishing and swimming along with a thoroughly western atmosphere and management we suggest you make Cinnabar Ranch your vacation choice.

BY ALL MEANS SPEND YOUR VACATION AND WEEKENDS AT CINNABAR RANCH . . . IN BEAUTIFUL PUTNAM COUNTY — BUT BUY YOUR WAR BONDS FIRST

. . . V

Member of the Eastern Dude Ranch Association

Reminiscent of the "Old West" guests enjoy a stage coach ride before the Sunday Rodeo. Cut at right—Before each ride, horses are taken to the brook where they may have their fill of water.

Many Boys from *Cinnabar Ranch* and Former Guests now in the Armed Forces

In the short space we have here it is hard to give you much news about all the boys listed here but it will give us pleasure to try locating any of them for you if you will drop us a line. There are also many girls who are now in the services but we have not heard from them yet so kindly excuse any omissions of them or of boys we do not know about yet.

Pvt. Vernon Walter, 407 T.S.S. Flight 1, Sheppard Field, Tex. ★ Cpl. Morris Miozza (Blackie), 30th Med. Reg. Co. G, Camp Barkley, Tex. ★ Pvt. Stanley Walter, Battery B 373, F.A.B.N., APO 447, Ft. Jackson, S.C. ★ Pvt. Kenneth Walter, Directorate Mobilization, Alymer Bldg, Ottawa, Can. ★ Thomas W. Brown, U.S.C.G. Sta., Mounted Div., Elkins Park, Penn. ★ Jack Ahearn, Bm. 1cl., Coast Guard Boat 60038, Pier 98, East River, N.Y. ★ Hal Reidinger, F 2 cl., USS J. T. Dickman, c/o Fleet Postmaster, N.Y.C. ★ Pfc. Alfred Bates, 278th Ord. Co., (M.M.) OUTC, M.O.D., Jackson, Miss. ★ John Boyhan, Platoon 80, 3rd Recruit Bn., Marine Barracks, Paris Island, S.C. ★ Ernest Clark, USCG, c/o Mach Shop, Fort Thompson, New London, Conn. ★ Lieut. L. W. Carnaroe, U.S.S. Nevada, c/o Postmaster, San Fransisco, Cal. ★ Edward Drews, C.P.O. 908 Amsterdam Ave., N.Y.C. ★ John Golden, R.M. 2 cl., U.S.C.G., P.C. 590, c/o Postmaster, San Fransisco, Cal. ★ Robert Brook Knapp, A.P.O. 680, c/o Postmaster, N.Y.C. ★ Pvt. Hannes Koops, 4th Platoon, Co. C, 14th Infantry, Ing. B.N. Camp Wheeler, Ga. ★ Pvt. Martin Kornhaas, Co. H, 6th T.R. Reg O.M., Camp Lee, S.C. ★ Lem Leavitt, Co. A, 28th TRG, Bn, Camp Croft, S.C. ★ Joseph Matysek, 531st School Squadron, Air Corps Basic Flying School, Army Air Base, Temore, Cal. ★ Ed May, Res. Squadron Group 1, Maxwell Field, Ala. ★ Pvt. Bill Odell, U.S. Army, 4th B.N., ERTC, Ft Belvin, Va. ★ Staff Sgt. Sam Pastorfield, Co. G, 417 Div., APO 76, Ft. Meade, Md. ★ Hank Zelner, RT 2cl., Radio Unit, Navy Yard, S.C. ★ Pvt. Russ Zimmer, H.G. Co. 98 Div., APO, Breckenridge Camp, Ky. ★ Pvt. R. H. Connelly, Co. G, 29th M.P. Bn, MPRTC (Bks. 2760) Ft. Riley, Kansas.

The above boys would appreciate a letter from anyone would care to write and the following are also in and we will try to secure their addresses for you.

Walter Akenburg, John Crone, Russell Edwards, Lieut. Robert Lehmann, Walter Miller, Frank Hogan, Harold Shaw, Walter Viebrock, Ralph Ferijo, Howard Hansis, Hugh Conway, Allan Dowdeswell, Eugene Otterson, Lieut. Alfred Birra, Bob Mahon.

CINNABAR DUDE RANCH NEWS

Earl Walter tests his stirrups for length on the ground, before saddling his bronc at the Rodeo. Lower—Hank Zelner and Ed Zieger shown coming through gate on one of the regular daily three hour rides.

A pretty guest is caught on the diving board, located on Cinnabar's beautiful lake, and below guest watches singing cowboy, Curly Atkinson, roll a cigarette from Bull-Durham.

The Virginia Reel is one of the most popular of the twice weekly square dances. Free beer is served at these old fashioned Hoe-downs. Cut at right—A busy dining room scene where guests enjoy the finest food, well prepared and served ranch style.

On the Fire

One thing we all should realize is we can always live on less when we have more to live for . . . It is good to hear Bob Knapp and Blackie Karmen will be home from their assignments in the Near East . . . One of my greatest failings is the neglect of writing letters to boys in the service and overseas so I hope it is not contagious . . . Our thanks to Foretop, daughter of Lorna Lindsley who presented us with a copy of her mother's new book about her experiences during the Spanish War and the invasion of France by the Germans . . . Connie and C. J. Walter spent several weeks in Miami this past winter where they encountered several guests who had been at the ranch in the past . . . Marge Dacci and Bill Stanfield were married the early part of this year . . . Silver Dawn the pure white albino colt is over a year old now and growing every day . . . George Gilmore, a very fine chef has replaced Charley Hoffman who has been in the army for some time now . . . Rodeos will continue to be a major event during the summer with guests participating to a greater extent than in past years . . . Cinnabar has contributed 10 cowboys to the armed forces as well as many others from different departments . . . Peggy and Curly Atkinson are the proud parents of a bouncing boy . . . Time flies fast and it doesn't seem possible Irene Walter and Tom Brown have been married so long . . . Earl Walter who has just turned 18 will soon be with the rest of the boys in some branch of the service . . . Vernon F. Walter, manager of Cimarron Ranch is now a sergeant in the mechanized cavalry at Fort Riley Kansas . . . Till we meet again—

ALLAN.

Food and Accommodations to be maintained at same high standard

CINNABAR has decided to lower the number of guests who may be accommodated this year to assure guests more private and semi-private rooms.

Food will be prepared in the same ranch style and there will be plenty to satisfy the most hearty appetite.

All the horses are in marvelous condition, ready to give everyone a good three hour ride through hills and valleys, that are a part of the Ranch. Picnic rides to Oscawanna Lake will be a weekly feature again this year.

CINNABAR DUDE RANCH NEWS

Time out to rest on the corral fence. Flash and Navajo press close to Allan and Charlotte Walter while Cinnabar Ranch makes a perfect background.

WE ARE PROUD TO ANNOUNCE OUR MEMBERSHIP IN THE EASTERN DUDE RANCH ASSOCIATION WHICH WAS FORMED IN DECEMBER 1942. ITS AIMS ARE THE JOINING OF REPUTABLE DUDE RANCHES IN THE EAST IN ONE COMMON BODY TO PROMOTE THIS TYPE RESORT ABOVE ITS PRESENT STATUS AS THE FOREMOST VACATION DESIRE OF PEOPLE IN THE EAST.

Girls like to learn everything there is to know about cowboys. Here Grace and Pat Morris are watching Mike Levelle roll a cigarette.

Guests are advised not to bring clothing which will not be used . . . especially dresses.

MANY FOLKS HAVE had the dude ranch urge in the past but have been reluctant to try it because they did not have what they considered the proper clothing. Any sports wear you might have will do for the length of your stay but in the event you would really like to go western Cinnabar's Western Store will be able to supply you with all the needed apparel. Levis, shirts, boots, ties and all the rest are available at all times for your inspection. The store also stocks soft drinks, saddles, blankets, bridles and souvenirs.

OUR CLIENTELE has been restricted to 75 this year to enable us to give you the utmost in comfort and congeniality. You will find our guests have been carefully selected and restricted to those who have a natural love for good horses and a genuine western atmosphere and hospitality. You will not be disappointed in their company.

RESERVATIONS are necessary and the $5 deposit you send to our New York office or to the ranch will apply to your bill. The ranch is easily accessible either by car or train.

IN ADDITION TO square dances, camp fires, roller skating, bowling, ping pong, rodeos, swimming, boating and other special events a baseball diamond is always ready to give exercise and enjoyment.

CINNABAR HORSES have been judged the finest dude ranch horses in the East and are always ready to give you a fine ride over the thousands of acres that the ranch occupies.

It has been Wisely Said that a change is as good as a rest—so Why not spend your Leisure Time at Cinnabar Ranch.

Meet the Walter Children

The Walters after Earl and Dottie Walter's Wedding

Vern Walter

Our oldest brother Vern was the official train greeter and host. He fit right into the ranch life and could step in for any absent worker. Vern loved the ranch and was a special person. In the war years, he was the first one in our family to enlist, joining the United States Air Force. He was stationed in Italy as an airplane mechanic. On one of his furloughs he met a special guest at the ranch named Margie Glynn. They were married after the war and lived in Waterbury, Conn.

Allan Walter

Allan was the manager of Cinnabar Ranch. He was a tall, handsome, intelligent man. He had the talent to run a tight ship, but still be your best friend. He wanted things done right, and if you worked for him you knew your duties. He wore debonair, tailored western clothing. He started Irene in the office and just let her find her way. He fell in love with one of our guests named Charlotte Schaaf. She had been injured in an accident and was spending the summer on the ranch. They were married and she became permanent help, and a member of our family.

Stanley Walter

Stanley had a perfect personality for the ranch life. Nothing stressed him out and his sense of humor was infectious. He was in charge of all the guest horse rides. He was aware of the temperament of each and every horse and knew how to match the right horse with the right guest. He was close to Mom and the nice little things he would do for her would put a smile on her face. Stan met his future wife at the ranch. Alyce was a lovely red headed girl, and did some modeling in the city. She commuted every day, so Stan would dote on her, bringing her morning coffee and taking her to the train. He dressed up pretty "spiffy" when it was time to pick her up in the afternoon. Stan served his country during World War II in the Army, deployed in the European Theater.

Iona Mae (Peggy) Walter

Peggy was named Iona Mae Walter at birth, but when she went to Detroit to work, she changed her name, and not many people even remember the name Iona. Peg was the shortest of all the girls, built very slim, and wore her Western clothes well. She was the hardest, fastest and most thorough worker the ranch ever had. We think she didn't want to spend any more time in drudgery than was needed. Peggy was the first in the family to order tailor made clothes. Her first bell-bottom gabardine suit pants were a beautiful blue-violet color. They had large flowers embroidered down the sides and on the bell-bottoms. Peggy married Joe Ferrante at the ranch. Joe was lured to the ranch for the rodeo days, and just never went home. Joe worked as a ranch hand. Joe married Peggy and they moved out to California, where Joe worked the local rodeos and worked in the movies. Joe was in the "Magnificent Seven" and the "Untouchables" movie.

Joe, Peggy and George Earl Ferrante as extras in the movie "Shane"

Kenneth Walter

Barbara and Kenneth Walter

Ken was one of the most honest, trustworthy, and thoughtful people around. He never stopped his education. He was quiet and somber looking, but he had the greatest dry sense of humor. He would say something with a straight face and just crack people up, that is if they caught the humor in what he was saying. He met his wife Barbara Mitchell at Cimarron. Barbara was an only child and her mom was sick, so she and Ken moved to New York City to be near her. He had no trouble finding a good position, but if it became apparent there was no way to advance in that company, he would get out his resume, decide where he would like to go, and he would move to a new job with better prospects. During the war he served in the U.S. Army.

Kenneth and C.J.

- 91 -

Irene Walter

Irene was the middle child of eleven. She worked at the ranch as hostess and office manager. Like the rest of the family, she participated in the weekly rodeos. Irene met her husband, Tom Brown, at the ranch. They were married in 1942, and they had six children. Tom Brown was an accountant in New York City and left this life to move to the ranch. Irene is one of the authors of this collection of memories.

Earl Walter

Earl worked in the stables at the ranch during his school years. He rode bareback broncos and saddle broncos in the rodeos and also took out "dude" rides whenever he could. Earl went into the US Army, and was happy to be assigned to the Calvary. He was glad when the war ended so he could get back to the ranch. We had a girl working for us named Dotty Cooper. He fell in love with her. They soon married and together went on the rodeo route. Dotty became a very talented trick rider and barrel racer. They traveled all over the country, even after their son Earl was born. That's a tough life for a family, because there isn't any guaranteed money, and you have to pay to enter a rodeo event. Earl and Dotty settled in upstate New York.

George Walter

George was only 14 years old when he was given his own stable to manage at the ranch. No other horses were as well taken care of and pampered as the ones in his barn. George had a lot of his mother's sweet disposition, had a shy grin, and was always very respectful. He too was active in the rodeo activities. He and Earl later went on to the RCA rodeo circuit. George went into the Army when he became of age, and returned to the ranch life as soon as he could. He met and married a young lady named Muriel Jackman. She also was a trick rider, and enjoyed the rodeo life as much as the rest of the family.

Maxine (Mackie) Walter

Maxine was a young girl whose smile could melt anyone's heart. When she was just a teenager, she was given a job as a waitress. That was her weekend job and she was very good at it. She also had her own horse and was very active in the weekly rodeos. In later years, she married Bill Schwerd. Bill would visit Cinnabar Ranch on weekends. He lived in Staten Island, the only son of a prominent doctor. He had the best horses and gear, and was a very natural, capable, and talented hand. In their early years Bill and Maxine toured the rodeo route. They moved upstate New York, and many members of our family moved up to that area when they were ready to settle down.

Doreen Walter

Doreen was a natural rider. C.J. bought her a trick riding saddle, gave her a large gentle horse, and told her to trick ride in the rodeos.

She learned the Hippodrome Stand, or standing on her horse at a lope around the arenas, and that was quite a picture. She learned other tricks, such as Vaulting, the Russian Drag and the Fender Drag. These were pretty impressive tricks for a teenager. She met Red Sloan in Florida at the Indian River Ranch. When we were all back at Cinnabar, we were surprised one day to see Red walk in. He had hitchhiked from Florida. C.J. gave him a job at the ranch, and he became a part of our family. Red and Doreen were married and they headed west to Pecos, Texas. Red and Doreen rode in rodeos in Pecos before moving to the northern part of California. It is because of Doreen's vivid memory, her preservation of all the ranch mementos, and deep desire to publish these memories that this book is being written.

Red Sloan in Cigarette Ad

Jeanette Walter

Jeanette Walter was a New Year Baby. As the first baby of the New Year in Regina, Saskatchewan, Connie and C.J. were given many gifts from the local merchants. All loved Jeanette, the youngest of the eleven. In 1934 she died of pneumonia at the age of four.

According to Irene and Doreen, this poem was written around 1943 by a "mild" acquaintance of Connie's she played cards with. Neither remembers the woman's name. Irene says she really loved Connie, which would have prompted her to write the poem.

The Walters

Connie's the flower
C.J. the stem
The heads of the family
Whose number is ten.
There's Kenneth and Vern
And Earl who chews cud
And Allen and Stan
Who's surely no dud.
George is the cowboy who tells tall tales,
Of blue snakes that fly and the lake that breeds whales.
There's Irene and Peggy
And the two who came last
Doreen and Maxine, they're growing up fast.
We love the whole bundle,
Tibby and I,
Boy! What a sandwich they'd make between rye!!

Vern is the oldest, he has wicked eyes
He makes lots of noise when with other guys
His plaid shorts become him, he makes the girls prance
While leading them through a whirlwind of a dance.
He whoops when he dances, ducks when he's mild
By all fair damsels he's ever beguiled.
No wonder they love him, both young and old
He's so meek and mild, and looks oh! So bold!!

Earl's the sophisticate, ogles the girls
And when his long body, at times he unfurls,
The lasses just oh-oh and think they're the ONE
While all the time he's just having fun.
He chews his tobacco with one pinch of snuff
When winds blowing right he disposes of stuff
To say the word "spit" would be not so proper,
To use it in public you'd come quite a cropper!
His eyes all a twinkle, his mouth in a grin
He's al fun and laughter, not one ounce of sin!!

Irene's the "looker" as I've heard it said
By her face and her figure the boys are all led
To Cinnabar Ranch they come as a dude
By tall ones and short ones she is ever wooed
But Tom has the niche where the others would be,
E'en though she has choice from A to Z!
Maxine's the cutie with blonde upturned curl
In a couple of years she'll give males a whirl,
Doreen's short pigtails are now right to wrench
By 16 they'll call her a fascinatin' wench.
At this tender age it's the pinball machine
But five years from now they'll make other girls green!

The following poem was written by Lila Walter, C.J's sister-in-law for the 1996 reunion:

The Walter Family

I've loved the Walter family
More than any else on earth
They've been there when I needed help
With comfort, cheer and mirth.

My husband, Loren James
Came to Thurman with his brother
To start and Eastern Dude Ranch
At that time there was no other.

Brother Vernon bought a farm
At the foot of Mountain Crane
He bought it from Earl Woodard
Who thought he'd do the same.

Vernon Walter was aggressive
His dreams came by the score
He always kept on seeking
Things he'd never done before.

For more responsibility
He married Lu Albreight
Eleven years his senior
At the time it seemed alright.

Lu did not want to live alone
In an old house isolated
Until she had some company
Back to Cleveland she retreated.

That's where I first met Loren
At historic house in town
But no one thought of history
Just danced there until dawn.

After that I seldom heard
Of news from the Thurman Town
In Glens Falls while in high school
Rumors came that Loren's gone.

He went back to Detroit
The place from which he came.
I think he stayed about a year
And then returned again.

From high school I'd graduated
Was attending Normal School
On Valentine's Day a card from him
Said, "What are you to do?"

From that day on we wrote
Until we met again
And after that reunion
We never felt the same.

We decided we would marry
Next year a baby came
To liven up the household
And bear the Walter name.

This song was written by Dotty Schaaf, Doreen and Maxine Walter after breaking a bunch of dishes in the kitchen at Cinnabar.

*Do you remember the night
When all the kitchen dishes fell?
C.J. came a running and he gave us hell.
Mackie and Finny ought to hang their heads in shame
Cause Harry and Dottie got the blame!*

*Hey look out, Hey look out,
Cried Red from the rear.
Hey look out is all you could hear..
So we picked up the dishes
and threw them down the chute,
Took a look at C.J. and then began to scoot.
Ivy and all the help and guests couldn't see,
What was going on in the pant-er-y.
this is the story of a happy Father's day,
That didn't turn out the proper way!*

**Irene and Doreen singing this song
While on a nostalgic visit to the Cinnabar Ranch site,
now the Continental Village community center and fire house**

Interesting People at the Ranches

Dixie and Roy Rogers and C.J. Walter

Many celebrities heard of our ranch and unless you knew who they were, you would never guess they were famous. That probably was why they loved the ranch and its warm atmosphere. They could just be themselves and enjoy their time away from the city.

Gene Autry, Lu Walter, Betty Cully

Gene Autry was a visitor at the ranches. We met him when he was the star of the Madison Square Garden Rodeo. He stopped in to meet our family at one of our rodeo parties at the Belvedere Hotel. Gene was such a low-keyed person, except for his beautifully tailored suit, you would think he was just one of our guys. C.J. felt like he had met a long time friend. He joined our table after the rodeo and stopped off at the ranch to visit. Doreen was bold enough to get his autograph and she still has the rodeo program he autographed for her.

In 1939, **Estelle Gilbert** bought a horse, which she boarded at Cimarron Ranch, near Peekskill, New York. She enjoyed life at the dude ranch and in 1940 accepted an office position at the ranch, which allowed her to spend more time riding. Work as a trail ride escort and riding instructor soon followed.

She became acquainted with Mike Hastings, who was a former rodeo performer and foreman of the ranch. She also worked at Gene Autry's Flying A Ranch near Ardmore, Oklahoma. Under the tutelage of Hastings, she was able to expand her riding abilities to include barrel racing and trick riding. Eventually she was able to rodeo competitively in these events during the late 1940s and early 1950s. During this period she became a dude ranch commuter, spending summers at the Cimarron Ranch in New York and winters at the Desert Willow Ranch near Tucson, Arizona. She was friend and companion to Mike Hastings until his death in 1965. She continued to live in the Peekskill, New York area, most often working as a waitress, until 1979, when she moved to California. She eventually settled in Yucaipa, where she became active in civic affairs, including the local animal shelter. She died at the age of 90 on August 17, 2003.

Joe Breckenridge was an artist and a life-long friend of C.J.'s. Any time he was down on his luck, he would drop in and stay until finally, after weeks of visiting, our mom would say, "Eleven children makes a house a bit crowded." However, Joe would turn up again after a couple of years. He arrived at Cinnabar and wowed our guests with his artistry. He would prop up an old door, put six squares of heavy cardboard on it and start painting, using brushes big enough to paint a house with! He would do the sky on all pictures, putting some white on his brush, and the clouds would appear. Then he would add a lake while he had that color on the brush; then some green for trees. It was just amazing to see six different scenes appear in less than an hour. He would sell the pictures and his work was done for the day. Even though he was making a living at the ranch, he never thought of paying for anything. And our father never thought of asking him to. Our dad thought he was "color," and he was. He sold many of his creations before they were even finished. He was a colorful character, and when he dressed in his fancy outfits, he was quite debonair.

Photo of Col. Jim Eskew taken in June, 1941

Colonel Jim Eskew was the gentleman who got C.J. into traveling rodeo shows. He was a rodeo producer and promoted shows all over the east. He stopped by Cinnabar Ranch and became good friends with C.J. He was quite impressed with our weekly rodeos and gave C.J. tips on where to get any specialty acts he needed. When the Colonel's business got too large, he asked C.J. to take over the surplus rodeos. This is how C.J.'s Traveling Rodeo started and it turned into a good sideline for the ranch. The Colonel was inducted into the Rodeo Hall of Fame in 1992 as a Rodeo producer.

Dotty Gunn was a fixture at our ranch; a young lady with an uncanny talent for photography. Our family is blessed with many pictures she took over the years. Dot is another person who just moved up to the ranch and stayed. My father didn't worry about how many extra mouths he fed, because he felt you couldn't put a price on "Color." Eventually he had one of the beautiful stone silos made into a photo lab and private quarters for her, and she ended up making a business out of a hobby she loved. Dotty took many of the pictures in this book. In later years she moved to Hollywood, California

Mike Hastings was a gnarly older man who was as sweet and kind as he was burley. He had been World Champion Bulldogger for many years. He was ready for a mellow life and enjoyed having three meals every day. He also loved being a part of our family. He always had a chaw of tobacco in his cheeks, and let each of us try a dab. Earl was the only one who thought this was a cool habit. Mike stayed at Cimarron Ranch when the family moved to Cinnabar. We still rode over to Cimarron to see him and get one of his bear hugs.

Candy Jones was a model for Harry Conover's Model Agency. She loved the ranch life and came up to do some advertising shoots for our brochure. She stayed for a while, but later married her boss, Harry Conover. After they divorced, she wrote a well-received book on the seamy side of modeling.

Jack LaFayette was only a teenager when he first came to Cinnabar. He would bring up his horse and trick ride in the rodeo. One newspaper called him, "A One Man Rodeo." Some of his feats were; The Slick Stand, Split the Neck, High Trooper, Reverse Trooper, and Suicide Drag. He would ride bareback broncs and trick ride. He stayed at the ranch for quite a while.

"Diamond" Ted Lewis was a true showman and became a good friend of C.J. He was the International Rifle and Pistol Shot Champion. His nickname came when he had diamonds implanted in all his front teeth. What a dazzling smile that man had! He too loved the atmosphere of Cinnabar and stayed as long as he could.

Paul Laune was a renowned illustrator and artist. He moved to Manhattan and wanted to find a place to ride horses. He found Cimarron Ranch and became good friends with Uncle Verne, Aunt Lu, and Mike Hastings. Verne asked him to design a mock western town for Cimarron Ranch. He designed "Westerntown," and was very pleased when it was completed. His mother, Seigniora Russell Laune, wrote a book called, "Sand in My Eyes," a story of their homesteading in the town of Woodward, Oklahoma.

Joe Phillips was only fifteen years old when he was first a guest at our ranches. His love of horses and showmanship was just being hatched. He spent much of his time at the ranch and it was there he learned calf roping, trick riding, whip cracking and trick-roping. Over time, and with experience, he developed 5 great specialty acts. He has been a showman with his horse and trained dogs for years, and is a tremendous hit wherever he appears with his animals. He has appeared in many movies, commercials and shows, and still performs today.

John Powers owned and operated the largest model agency in New York City. He brought up some models for a picture shoot for our ranch brochure. He loved the ranch atmosphere. It was so unlike the busy life in the city. He lost his girlfriend to a ranch hand, when she stayed on and became a chambermaid. John later married and bought a horse and spent much time at Cinnabar.

Roy Rogers was our guest of honor at several of our Madison Square Garden Rodeos and joined us for the after-Rodeo parties. We have a great photo of him with his first wife and our family. He was a gracious fellow, and enjoyed being treated as a friend instead of a star.

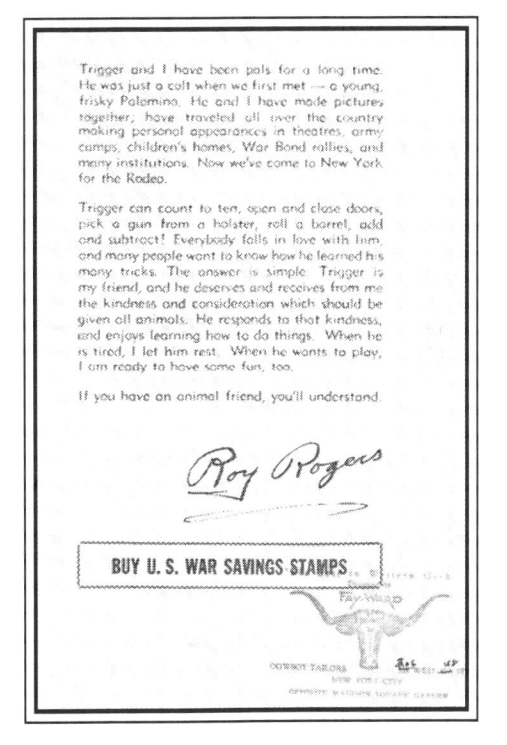

- 107 -

Seated: Dixie Rogers, Connie and C.J. Walter, and Roy Rogers' publicity agent
Middle Row: Herman Fredericks, Earl Walter, Ingrid Severied,
Roy Rogers, Doreen Walter, Harry Tompkins, Irene Walter
Standing in back: Jean, Dottie and Maxine Walter, Tom Brown

Harry Tompkins came to the ranch wanting to ride the horses. C.J. told him if he wanted to ride, he had to work, so this lad came over every day after school and on weekends. He was probably the most natural horseman we met with perfect balance and good hands. He rode rodeo when we had our Sunday shows and was never bucked off a bull. He later went on to be the National Champion Bull Rider for many years. He was a gentleman at all times. When he came home, he was ready to enter the Madison Square Garden Rodeo, sponsored by the ranches. He has been inducted into several "Cowboy Hall of Fames."

1948
5th All Around $17,296
4th Bareback $5,982
Bull Riding Champion $11,313

1949
4th All Around $18,875
5th Bareback $5,336
Bull Riding Champion $13,290

1950
3rd All Around $25,891
Bull Riding Champion $19,213

1951
5th All Around $16,321
2nd Bulls $10,920

1952
All Around Champion $30,934
Bareback Champion $$14,152
Bull Riding Champion $16,783

1953
4th All Around $22,599
2nd Bareback Champion $12,163
3rd Bulls $10,436

1954
6th All Around $23,834
5th Bulls $11,705

1955
4th All Around $23,060
3rd Bulls $12,496

1956
6th All Around $21,523
2nd Bulls $13,401

1957
7th All Around $21,528
3rd Bareback $11,330
3rd Bulls $10,198

1958
4th All Around $23,953
4th Bareback $12,210
3rd Bulls $11,743

1959
13 Bulls $7,277

1960
All Around Champion $32,522
2nd Bareback $15,379
Bull Riding Champion $17,143

1961
11th All Around $18,395
11th Bareback $8,141
6th Bulls $10,253

1965
10th All Around $20,357
12th Bareback $9,223
6th Bulls $11,334

1967
13th Bulls $9,987

Chet Tyler was a true entertainer; he could keep an audience happy all night. He and his wife enjoyed being at the ranch, and he could sing and pick a guitar with anyone. He was a fine person and an asset to our ranches. Chet Tyler appeared in several Cinnabar rodeos. He is a star of great ability. He has an affable personality, with an engaging smile. Chet has fulfilled radio engagements for stations far and wide.

Bill Vogel was another ranch character. He was born in Minnesota and raised in California. He came to the ranch as a guest and stayed. He was a successful film producer but soon divorced and the majority of his money went for alimony. He told C.J. he would work for room and board, because without any income, he didn't have to pay any alimony. He was happier than he had been in years. Some of the movies he had a hand in producing were; "Test Pilot", "The Good Earth", "Sequoia" and "The Lost World" in 1919, and "The Sheik" in 1924. At the time he was at the ranch, he was working with Transfilm of New York and was still a successful man. He loved the ranch and would do anything C.J. asked him to do. He became a real character with a beard and large western hat, and the guests loved visiting with him. He assisted C.J. with the rodeos and took on the character of "Wild Bill Cody."

This famous person was not a guest at one of the Walter ranches, but when C.J. was managing the Lost Wilderness guest ranch in Massachusetts, John F. Kennedy made a visit. C.J. wasn't awed by his stature, but our mom Connie really was impressed. She became a Democrat that day. She followed his career from then on and on the day when he died so tragically, she grieved like she lost one of her own children.

Shown here in his early twenties, Fay Ward poses in some fancy chaps.

Fay Ward was an amazing tailor responsible for all the fancy "dude" clothes worn by the family and guests. Fay Ward was a cowboy, bronc rider, and rodeo hand who in later years opened a small shop in New York City. Different members of the family went to New York to be fitted and pick up their outfits - but Doreen remembers being fitted in the Cinnabar Ranch square, in front of all the guests.

Be in style in western garments designed by America's leading and only cowboy tailor — *Fay Ward*

Fay Ward may have been the only real cowboy ever to design duds for dudes.

Pictures courtesy of Persimmon Hill Magazine
Editor: M.J. Van Deventer
1977 article by Keith Walters

A few of
the outfits
made and
designed by
Fay Ward

Bess Johnson was a famous star of the radio soap operas. She also was in All My Children, one of the original soap operas. She too fell for the ranch life and had a lovely home built on Cinnabar's property, keeping her horse at the ranch.

Lowell Thomas was a radio announcer C.J. always listened to on the radio. When he visited Cinnabar, he loved the idea that up there he was just an ordinary person. He loved talking to C.J. and did several write-ups about him and our ranch. When Cinnabar was sold, C.J. looked at his estate as a future ranch sight.

Texas Tommy was a rodeo performer at the ranches. His horse was called Baby Rob and he performed tricks.

Other Ranches

**1947 - Herman Fredericks, trick rider in front of
the Walter Ranch, Garrison, New York**

- ★ 1932 - Ski-Hi Ranch, Athol, New York
- ★ 1940–1944 - Indian River Ranch, New Smyrna Beach, Florida
- ★ 1944 - Double U Ranch, Tucson, Arizona
- ★ 1946 - Calico Ranch, Woodstock, New York
- ★ 1946 - The Walter Ranch, Garrison On Hudson, New York
- ★ 1949 - Timberlane Ranch, East Jewett, New York
- ★ 1952 - Calico Ranch, Wurtsboro, New York
- ★ 1952 - Au Sable Guest Ranch, Gaylord, Michigan
- ★ 1953 - Lost Wilderness Ranch, New Boston, Massachusetts
- ★ 1955 - Flying W Ranch, Newtown, Connecticut

Ski-Hi Ranch - 1932

Thurman, New York

This lovely ranch in the Adirondacks of New York State was one of the earliest dude ranches in the east. Vernon F. Walter was the owner and operator and, until his death in 1963, he was a pioneer of the dude ranch industry.

Vern and his wife Lulu purchased this land in 1931. The Guest Ranch was opened for business on the 25th of May that year. When they started the Sky-Hi ranch they had no electricity and used kerosene oil lamps. There were no indoor bathroom facilities. The atmosphere of the place was warm and charming. The accommodation rates at Ski-Hi started at $45.00 weekly, with an extra $10.00 charge for riding. In 1933 they built 2 log cabins just west of the main house on a rise. Each had a fireplace and two bedrooms.

Vern was unique because he had a knack of knowing how to treat New York City people. He introduced them to a way of life never before imagined by these folks. He was a unique, charming, and handsome man, who made this type of vacation spot so very successful. A guest at one of our ranches stepped out of one lifestyle and into another. Many of these guests actually cried when their vacation was over. They often became regulars and visited the ranches whenever possible.

Main ranch house at Ski-Hi Ranch

Vern was careful to buy safe, sound, well broken-in horses, hiring good help to teach the new dudes how to ride. He served very good food and had clean comfortable accommodations and caring personnel. Horse back riding was truly a new and unique sport in the area. A 3000-acre State Park surrounded Ski-Hi ranch, so there was unlimited riding trails. A person riding horseback could see Mount Marcy, the highest peak in the Adirondacks, Whiteface, and Haystack. Blue Mountain and the Green Mountains of Vermont, the Berkshires of Massachusetts, and many sparkling, hidden lakes could also be seen. This amazing vista was a seventy-five mile view of unsurpassed beauty. Business was good and this was the beginning of a life long career for Vern Walter. Loren Walter was right hand man for his brother Verne when they first opened Sky-Hi Ranch. He was the younger brother of C.J. and Vern, and was one of the ranch hands. He and his wife Lila lived in the Athol area. Vern's older sister Ann took three months leave from her job in Detroit to wait tables, make the beds, and everything else that needed doing. This was the beginning of family participation in all of the Walter dude ranches. Vern left this ranch in 1938 to open Cimarron Ranch.

Ski-Hi Ranch

THURMAN, NEW YORK
WARREN COUNTY

An Ideal Vacation Spot

SKI-HI
is a
Hunter's Paradise

- You can shoot a deer from the front porch of the main ranch house.
- Hunting parties have the sole use of the ranch property. A guide is also available.
- Make your reservations as early as possible.

THEODORE H. RICHTER
(OWNER AND MANAGER)

SKI-HI RANCH
THURMAN, N.Y.

RATES

Per Week — $45.00
$55.00 (with horses)
Children under 12 years — Half Rate

This includes everything.
There are NO EXTRAS at SKI-HI

During June and September the above rates are $5.00 less.

How To Get To Ski-Hi

From New York there are three ways in which to come to the ranch.

1. BY BUS—all the way to Warrensburg (Adirondack Trailways or Greyhound).
2. BY TRAIN—to Saratoga Springs and change for Thurman Station, N.Y. on the D & H Railway.
3. BY CAR—follow U.S. route 9 to Warrensburg and turn left on route 418 then follow the "SKI-HI" ranch signs.

The ranch car will meet the bus and train but time of arrival must be known well in advance. Should you desire any further information write to SKI-HI RANCH and your inquiry will receive a prompt reply.

An Unusual Vacation That Will Long Be Remembered

Brochures of Ski-Hi Ranch after Vern Walter left for Cimarron Ranch

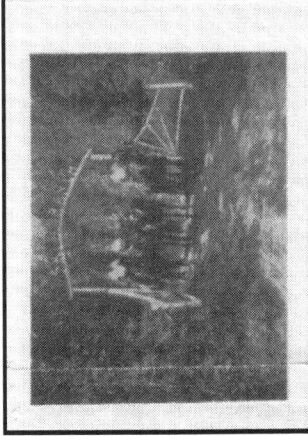

COME TO SKI-HI FOR YOUR FAVORITE VACATION.

Participate in active sports or relax and loaf to your heart's content.

- SKI-HI Ranch is situated 19 miles from Lake George, 2,000 feet high in the Adirondack Mountains and is at the foot of Crane Mountain, which towers 1,600 feet above the ranch. This location provides a marvelous view and a delightful cool climate.

- Hikes and trail riding over the ranch property and adjoining State Park keeps are marvelous at nature's handiwork.

- We have double cabins with joint bath accommodating four persons, a lodge with eleven bed rooms, recreation room and baths which will accommodate 21 persons. The main building includes dining room, kitchen and living room with recreation facilities.

- No formalities will be found at the ranch but home-like surroundings, well prepared food, finest of beds, ample entertainment can be enjoyed by all.

- Our planned program includes approximately 20 hours per week riding picnics, square dances, swimming, mountain climbing and rodeos. Other activities includes badminton, archery, rifle practice, fishing ping-pong and horse shoe pitching.

- The corral is adequately stocked to insure riding requirements and is under the direct supervision of the ranch owner. Riding parties on all planned rides will be under the supervision of a capable cowboy. Horses may also be rented by the hour.

- Excellent golf courses and tennis courts are within driving distance but we know you will not stray away from the activities of the ranch for either one.

- Protestant and Catholic Churches are near.

FOOD: Good home cooked meals are served family style. Great variety of fresh vegetables and choice cuts of meat are served in abundance. We know what this mountain air does to appetites, and we are prepared for them at every meal. Delicious pies and cakes make your desserts a treat.

CLOTHES: No dressy clothes are needed. Bring sports and riding clothes, bathing suit, a warm jacket or sweater, comfortable walking shoes, flashlight and camera.

RESERVATIONS: In as much as only 25 guests can be accommodated it will be necessary for reservations to be made well in advance. A deposit of $5.00 per person is required. This amount is not extra but applies to your account.

Indian River Guest Ranch
1940 - 1944

New Smyrna Beach, Florida

Vern Walter in front of Indian River Ranch sign

The Indian River Guest Ranch was the winter home of Vern and Lu Walter, and several members of the Walter family. This ranch was on the site of a boy's school that operated in New Smyrna Beach in 1929. This ranch had a main house and many small cabins, deep in palm, pine and fruit. trees The ranch had a large cabana on the beach, about a half hours ride from the ranch. The guests would ride to the beach, and spend the day riding, and relaxing. The cabana had a wrap-around deck, perfect for sunny days. The horses would be moved from Cimarron to Florida by truck and trailer or by train each winter.

**Vern, Lu and Irene Walter and guest
Riding in the Orchard at Indian river Ranch**

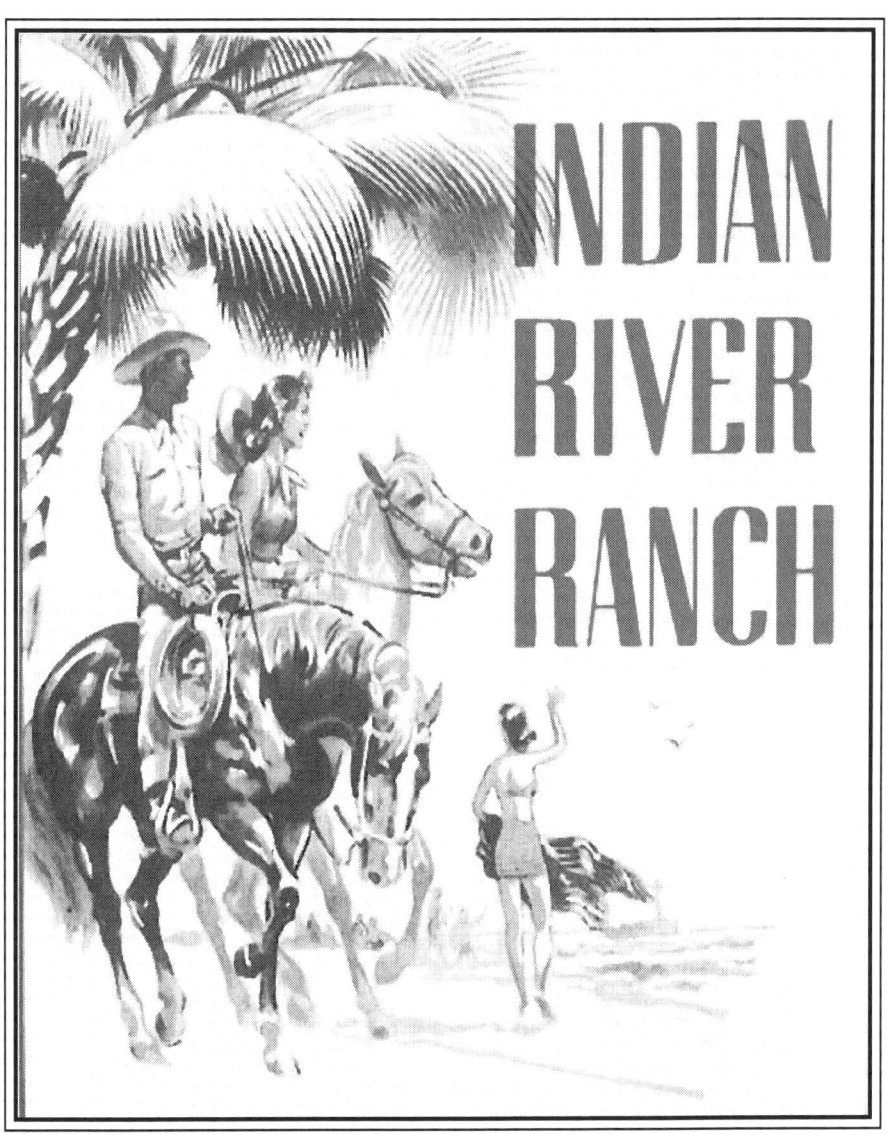

This is part of a three ranch brochure for Cimarron Ranch,
Cinnabar Ranch and Indian River Ranch
Very few pictures were taken at the ranch property, as
the palm trees made it very dark, and nicely cool.

NEW SMYRNA BEACH, FLORIDA

And when winter comes! — Florida calls you to our Indian River Ranch at New Smyrna Beach by the sea ... and don't you believe Florida isn't great dude ranch country ... nowhere will you find such riding trails, hard packed sand and not a stone in a hundred miles. You can ride to your heart's content at any gait you choose

43

through an ever changing maze of scenery in an air that is invigorating to both horse and rider . . . and when the sun beats down you will hie yourself to our beach cabana directly on the ocean, a ten minute drive by car or an hour on horseback to bask in the sun, loll on the pure white sands or take a plunge in the frothy surf, warmed by the great Gulf Stream. Around the

44

ranch you will find an air of lazy plantation life, a pleasant change from the hustle and bustle of busy city life. Accommodations are in a main lodge or private cabins scattered snugly in the pines to insure privacy. The Indian River Ranch will open about December 1st this year. Further information and rates will be furnished upon request.

45

Double U Ranch - 1944
Tucson, Arizona

C.J., Connie, Peggy, Stanley and Alyce would spend the winters working in Tucson, Arizona at the Double U Ranch. One story Stanley told me still makes me laugh. At the Double U Ranch, one of his jobs was to meet the guests at the airport. He told us of two ladies who flew in from Chicago. Stan showed them to their rooms and wished them a good night. In the morning, he was surprised to see them quite upset and asked them what the matter was. They said they were checking out, and he asked them why. They said they were kept awake all night by the coyotes howling and they didn't like wild animals. Stan laughed and smoothly told them that the management played that record at night just for western atmosphere! His little "white lie" worked, and they stayed to have a great vacation.

Publicity Photos from the Double U Ranch

- 123 -

Pool at the Double U Ranch

Main Building – Double U Ranch

**Stanley Walter setting out to
Pick up guests at the airport**

Calico Ranch - 1946
Woodstock, New York

Irene on one of the calico horses the ranch was known and named for.

C.J. Walter and a guest relaxing on the dinner bell at Calico

Bill Stanfield trick roping at Calico Rodeo ring

Peggy, Dottie, Tom, C.J., Connie Irene and Pam

Calico Ranch was a dream come true for three young couples after the war: Tom and Irene Brown, Bill Stanfield and his wife Marge, and Jack Ahern and his wife Eileen. We didn't have much money, but a lot of pride and ambition. We were fortunate to find an empty estate, near Woodstock, New York. The main house had been badly burned by fire, and renovation and cleaning was the first chore for all six. When we were finished, this main house was beautiful; all the real wood walls were refinished and exquisite. An interesting feature of this large home was the wide stairway that went to the second floor, several lovely large bedrooms there, and a huge bathroom, wheel chair assessable. It was said that Franklin Delano Roosevelt had been a guest of the former owners, and this accommodation was made for him. The Ranch had nice stables and new corrals and hitching posts were erected immediately. A fine string of riding horses, all pintos, was purchased, hence the name Calico Ranch. There was another large ranch building that was made into the office, bar, kitchen and dining room. These six enterprising young people were the prime employees; however, we slowly got hands to help with the horses and rides. The three ladies did all the female work. This was a labor of love and the reward was being owner/ operators. When Tom and Irene were expecting their third child, and their first daughter was ready to start school, they sold their partnership, and the Brown family moved to Oklahoma to farm.

Tom Brown, Jake Kornhouse, Marge Stanfield, Eileen and Jack Ahern watching Bill Stanfield trick roping.

Ranch before Renovations

Rodeo Field at Calico Ranch

Main House at Calico

Calico Dining Room

Bill and Marge Stanfield Practicing

Square Dancing Club

The Kingston Daily Freeman
May 22, 1947

Calico Ranch to Open Memorial Day on 'Range' at Lake Hill

Fun for All Ages Is Plan of Brown, Ahern Partnership

Woodstock, May 22 – Last minute preparations are being made at Calico Stock and Guest Ranch for the opening of the summer season on Memorial Day. The chief attention is being put on the main ranch house where the most extensive alterations are being made. This house will be remembered as the old Daley house which was partially damaged by fire many years ago.

Calico is beautifully situated in Mink Hollow, at Lake Hill, and is owned by Tom Brown and Jack Ahern. These two young men are westerners who have worked on many ranches in Arizona, North Dakota and Montana before coming East in 1940. Although their backgrounds are similar, they did not meet until they arrived at Cinnabar Ranch in Peekskill, where they worked at rodeos. A mutual regard since their first meeting, has developed over the years, resulting in their present joint business enterprise.

During the war Tom and Jack served in the U.S. Coast Guard, and enlisted at the same time. Much to their surprise, their first assignment was that of training war dogs and horses. Tom continued in the work until his discharge, but Jack was soon transferred to the "Monticello" where he served as boson's mate.

Tad is Roundup Hand

It is easy to believe that Tom was one of the few men in the Coast Guard who trained both horses and dogs, when you see Tad, a black and tan German Shepard dog, in action rounding up the horses and keeping them where they belong. Without a word of suggestion from his master, he goes about his job in a most efficient manner.

One of the new features at Calico this year will be the "Coke Bar" for the children. This is a large attractive room with a juke box where the young people may enjoy their own fun while resting between rides.

Calico was chosen for the name of the ranch because of the full string of spotted horses acquired for their opening last summer. A beautiful Dalmatian, christened Calico, completed the picture. A remark by an old dude rancher will best describe the string of 35 horses now at Calico, when he said, "As good a dude ranch string as I have ever seen, extremely well broke, good manners and willingness."

Weekly Square Dances

The first of the Saturday night square dances was held last Saturday evening. These dances will continue each week throughout the summer. George Harcourt and his Calico Ramblers furnish the music for these jolly events.

Rodeos will be held at the Lake Hill Arena Sunday afternoons with the Ranch guests participating. Every third week there will be a professional show.

Because of the interest on the part of many Woodstock and Kingston boys, a roping club is being considered for this season. In the conduct of this business, the duties of manager fall on the shoulders of Tom Brown, while those of corral boss are Jack Ahern's responsibility.

Wives are Great Assets

The story of Calico would not be complete without mentioning the power behind the thrones, otherwise known as Irene Brown and Eileen Ahern, who are great assets to their husbands in this business venture. These attractive and enthusiastic young women are both excellent riders and largely responsible for the comfortable accommodations their guests enjoy.

The kind, gentle and understanding manner Tom Brown displays in working with children has made him somewhat a hero to the horse-loving young people in Woodstock and vicinity.

THE SUNDAY NEWS, SUNDAY, JUNE 1, 1947

Calico Ranch Rodeos Again This Summer

Some of the Calico Ranch rodeo hands—Tom Brown, Jack Altern Tex Tyler, Bill Standfield, Jack Kornhaus

Memorial Day weekend finds Calico Ranch in full swing and beginning its second year in Woodstock. The Calico Ranch boys have made a warm place for themselves in the community and Tom Brown, the manager is a popular hero with the younger set. They unanimously voted him President of the Woodstock Riding Club which boasts a membership of girls and boys from 10 years up. Tom has put in a "Coke Bar" for them, with ping-pong, etc., at the Ranch along with the "Rodeo Bar" for the older folks. Contractors working on the main house of the Ranch expect to have it finished by July 1st and there are other improvements.

In addition to the Ranch is Tom Brown's father-in-law C. J. Walter, owner of the former Cinnabar Ranch at Peekskill, who is spending the Summer and looking around for a new location for Cinnabar.

The Calico Ranch boys will hold rodeos again this year. Starting on June 15, one will take place every three weeks along with a guest rodeo every week up at the arena at Lake Hill where cheering crowds get hair-raising thrills when the Western wranglers on their Calico pintos did trick riding last Summer.

Tom Brown is proud of the new string of horses and says that, due to the steady increase of horse enthusiasts, additional stock has been shipped in for re-sale.

For guests at Calico Ranch every hour if full. Right after Memorial Day weekend, square dances will be given every Thursday night.

Shirts, jeans and boots are the thing to wear. Hay rides, swimming, hunting and fishing, and hours of riding on miles of trails add up to a marvelous time in one of the most beautiful spots in the Catskill Mountains.

Woodstock Proposed

Calico Ranch Gives Woodstock Old West Flavor

About five miles from Woodstock postoffice, as the crow flies, in the hills above Mink Hollow, things are happening. The Calico Ranch is there and takes actual seeing for believing that something so completely out of Montana can be so near and come so quietly. We see the ranch wagon, black with a white silhouette of a cowboy and bucking broncho on the side and we have noticed, casually, the quiet courteous men in Western clothes going about their marketing in the village, but it gave no clue to the big enterprise they had embarked on. Woodstock had about everything except a ranch and now it is to have one of the most beautiful ones in the East. They expect to be ready for fifty or sixty guests this summer. Six were there over the weekend.

Tom Brown, Jack Ahearn, Bill Stanfield with their wives, are the joint owners. They are all vets of World War II and the three couples are a delightful group of lean, strong, long-legged young people. They have the same friendly ways, making you feel immediately welcome. There is breezy, intelligent talk and laughter, a sense of warm hospitality. They do all the work, helped out by two or three hands for work around the stables, and they keep things humming. Guest rooms are being put in readiness, buildings remodeled and built, and horses, horses everywhere. Thirty-two of them are spotted horses, and so the name "Calico Ranch." Even the dog is spotted Dalmatian.

Tom Brown and I stood looking across the sloping field. The swimming pool gleamed blue and the woods were touched with a mist of spring green. The mountains beyond seemed very high with a breath-taking line against the sky, a line so different from any I had seen in many years of Woodstock that I exclaimed 'it isn't possible this is Woodstock! I didn't dream our hills could look that way." Tom nodded, "this is the only place I know anywhere in the East that (Continued on Page 13)

looks the way people expect a ranch to look."

It is spacious, exhilarating, and one feels a thousand miles from the long sweep of hills around the Woodstock Valley. In a different world.

To reach Calico Ranch, you drive to Lake Hill turning right at Jule Simpson's Trading Post on the Mink Hollow road. About four miles along, the road forks, and the upper fork on the left leads to the ranch about a mile up the hill on a dirt road. There you are. Wide and open under the sky is the ranch. A sense of vigorous, contented outdoor life is all about.

CALICO RANCH
"HOME OF THE PINTO HORSES"
110 miles (3 hrs.) from N. Y. C.
Riding, Swimming, Rodeos, Square Dances,
All Sports.   Good Food.   Booklet H.
P. O. Box 386, WOODSTOCK, N. Y.
Tel.: N. Y. Office, BU. 8-3757

CALICO
Stock & Guest Ranch
Woodstock, N. Y.
"Home of the Pinto Horse"
Unlimited Riding, packtrips, rodeos, Western cocktail lounge. All sports. Special week-end festivities. Write or phone for Booklet.   C. J. WALTER, Ranch Manager
Woodstock 2-F-24

Three young "Dude Wranglers" invite you to a REAL WESTERN VACATION at

CALICO STOCK AND GUEST RANCH

Vacation the Western Way

P. O. Box 386
Woodstock, New York

"HOME OF THE PINTO HORSE"
110 mi. from N. Y. C.—Unlimited riding, sports, swimming, dancing, rodeos—true friendly Western atmosphere. Transp. to all churches.
MAKE RESERVATION NOW

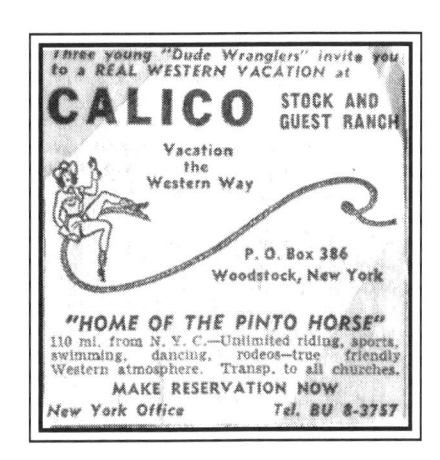

New York Office   Tel. BU 8-3757

Calico horses in front of Guest Cottage

Calico Ranch Rodeo Poster and singing ranch hands

Linda and Jerry Walter, Friends of the Walters but no relation, started their Susie Q Smith cartoon at the ranch

Walter Ranch - 1946

Garrison On Hudson, New York

Main House, Walter Ranch

When Cinnabar Ranch closed in 1946, the Walter family took over the operation of the Manitoa Ranch in Garrison, New York. This ranch was operated much like Cinnabar Ranch, with riding, rodeos, and the friendly, warm Walter hospitality.

One of the guest cottages at the Walter Ranch

WALTER RANCH NEWS

The traditional climax of The Grand Entry at a Cinnabar Rodeo. You'll see and cheer the same at the Walter Ranch this season.

Ranch Christmas

There is always a lull at the Ranch just before Christmas. It gives us an opportunity to do our Christmas shopping and gift wrapping. Our Christmas tree is almost hidden from view by an embankment of presents for the children. These are distributed Christmas Eve. Christmas is a quiet happy day and the dinner brings the whole family together at a long table. Evening comes and departs. The children are put to bed and soon after we follow. The day after Christmas (we call it boxing day) is tinged with sadness because we sense that something good leaves when Christmas goes. By night time we are preoccupied again preparing for the exciting new Years Party.

No one here says "Christmas is not like it used to be" whatever else may change, Christmas remains the same.

Rodeo Field Under Construction for Next Summer's Rodeos

A fine new Rodeo Field is under construction. Cedar posts have been selected and brought down from the northern part of the state. This field will be as large as any we have had and will be equipped with flood lights for night performances.

Rodeos will be staged at the ranch at least once a week during the summer. Certain events will be open to guests only.

"C. J." also expects to show his full scale rodeo in several eastern towns and cities this coming Spring and Summer. He has some definite bookings and a few tentative engagements lined up.

Our rate schedule has remained the same for the past two years. We intend to hold to these rates this year if possible. Our rates will be promptly reduced if there is a general price decline.

If you are planning to spend your vacation with us we advise you to make an early reservation. This will absolutely insure you against any price increase and you will benefit if rates are reduced. We will not require a deposit until later in the year.

PLEASE RESERVE EARLY FOR ANY HOLIDAY WEEKEND

RATES Per person including Room, Meals, Entertainment, and Horseback Riding.	Member of Eastern Dude Ranch Association		* Rate varies according to size and location of room and bath facilities.	
	Length of Stay	Girls' Dormitory or Men's Bunkhouse	Double or Twin Rooms *	Private Room *
WEEKLY For Full Week	7 Full Days	65.00	70.00 to 90.00	75.00 to 95.00
WEEKDAY SPECIAL Five Full Days	5 Full Days	47.00	50.00 to 63.00	53.00 to 72.00
WEEK-END Friday After Supper Sunday After Supper	2 Full Days	23.50	27.00 to 35.00	30.00 to 38.00
SATURDAY After Breakfast To Sunday After Supper		21.50	25.50 to 33.00	28.00 to 35.00
SATURDAY After Lunch To Sunday After Supper		20.00	23.00 to 30.50	25.50 to 32.50
SATURDAY Before Supper To Sunday After Supper		16.50	20.00 to 27.00	22.50 to 29.50
DAILY WEEK-DAY RATE		11.00	11.50 to 15.00	12.50 to 16.00

Non Riders may deduct $10.00 Weekly from above rates.

TELEPHONES GARRISON 550 & 977 — LONGACRE 3-2127

These fine horses will give you enjoyable rides

DINING ROOM—And after the ride—plenty of food served ranch style.

Trading Post News

We expect to sell everything western in the Trading Post. Guests coming to the ranch for the first time will be able to purchase a complete ranch outfit at a reasonable cost.

Our clothing stock will include boots, frontier pants, shirts, levi jackets and pants, hats, neckerchiefs and ties. We will cater to the horse by featuring saddles, bridles, sugar lumps, carrots and apples.

SPECIAL NOTE: Levis are still in short supply. We will send them to you postpaid for $4.00 per pair. Let us know the size you desire or give us your waist measure. Please remit with order.

New Year's Weekend

It was a happy time for all at our New Year's Party. This despite the weather. We sent rides out every day during the blizzard weather and hitched up our cutter a couple of times. We went to Bear Mountain Park for skiing and tobogganing. The square dances on Wednesday and Saturday gave the orchestra and the dancers a real workout.

Charlie and Ollie Mich of Bridgeport organized a party of almost thirty to come up to the New Year's Party. They were a good bunch and we were glad to have them with us. It continues an old Cinnabar tradition.

THE RANCHIEST RANCH IN THE EAST

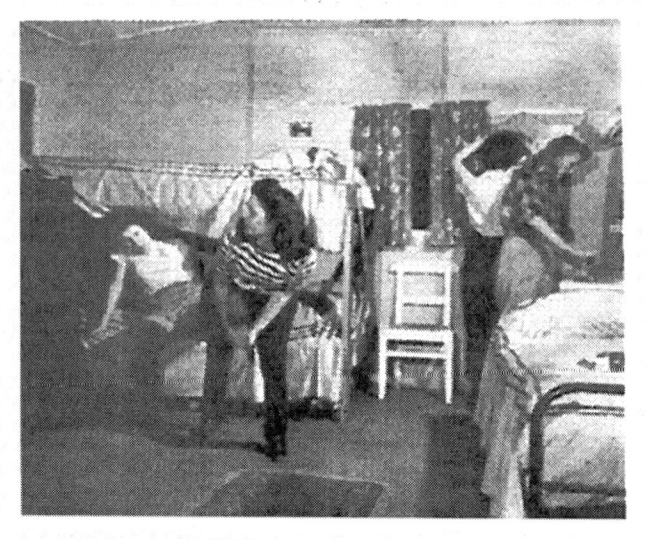

GIRLS DORM—The girls dorm and the men's bunkhouse are the most popular accommodations—and also the most reasonable

Who's Who at the Walter Ranch

Bill Schwerd is a well built, blond haired cowboy who hails originally from Staten Island where his father is a prominent physician. He was born about twenty-five years ago and has been trick riding almost half his life.

In January 1943 Bill entered the Marine Corps and saw a good deal of rough action. He helped to write Marine History in the Solomon and Marshall Islands which were in the headlines a few years ago. He fought on Guam and Iwo Jima and picked up a little shrapnel but didn't bother to claim a purple heart because he didn't know then that it would count towards the Discharge every serviceman looked forward to.

After demobilization Bill rodeoed with several well known outfits including Jim Colburn's, Jim Eskew's, the S. M. S. Outfit and C. J. Walter's Rodeo. At C. J.'s Oneonta Rodeo Bill devised a clever finale which called for him to make a perilous climb up a moving flagpole carried by two mounted riders and to release a hidden flag.

A year or so ago Bill married Maxine Walter. They now have a very nice boy and have settled down til the next rodeo.

Vern, the oldest Walter boy is living in Waterbury and is our connecticut representative. Allan is managing Panorama Ranch near Poughkeepsie. Irene Walter Brown helps her husband Tom run Calico Ranch near Woodstock, N. Y.

Out Where the Rest Begins

"Why is a well-built girl like a three ring circus?"
"I'll bite. Why is she?"
"Because a man doesn't know where to look first."

A staring cowboy always irks a young woman—especially if he's staring at another woman.

Cautious Bulldogger: "What time do you have to be home, girlie?"
49th St. Belle: "How much money have you got?"
"Five hundred dollars."
"Friday."

Query: Is it proper for a girl to wear men's levis at your ranch?
Answer: Yes, if the end justifies the jeans.

Range Law Cypress Hills

There is no need for many laws
To keep the Rangeland straight,
Or a book to keep them in because
There are only six or eight.

The first one is the Welcome sign
Wrote deep in Western hearts,
My camp is yours and yours is mine
In all Cow-Country parts.

Treat with respect all womankind,
Same as you would your sisters,
Take care of neighbor's strays you find,
Don't call cowboys "Misters"

Shut pasture gates when passing through,
And taken all in all,
Be just as rough as pleases you
But never mean and small.

Talk straight, shoot straight,
But never break your word to man or boss.
Just really kill a rattlesnake
Don't ride a sore-back horse.

You don't need laws or pedigree
To live the best you can,
And that is all it takes to be
A cowboy or a man.

HARRY OTTERSON
T J Ranch, Climax, Sask.

COFFEE TALK

About ten times a day the ranch hands stop all work to have a cup of coffee. The reason for this is not because they like coffee but the occasion interrupts the working day and gives everyone a chance to talk about saddles, trails, other ranches, and about our guests. It is in these talks that the good and bad points of each of our guests are given a going over. When you come up join the coffee table and contribute your bit to the coffee talk.

One of our first guests at the new ranch was Bill Proulx and he's been up several times since. Ruth Nelson is also a frequent weekender. Katherine Davis, Lois McQuilty, Valerie Young Catherine Brigley and Eleanor Kraker were a nice party. John Starrin and his son dropped in for lunch and a ride.

Carl Stenzler and his wife Erna spent a few days with us. They did a lot of sightseeing. Erna gave Stan a lesson in coffee making he won't soon forget. Mary Lewicki of the Martha Owen Agency was up—we appreciate the backing Martha Owen's agency has always given our ranches. Betty White agency has also done well by us.

THE SECRETARY OF WAR
WASHINGTON

2 October 1946

Dear Mr. and Mrs. Walter:

My attention has been called to the fact that you have six sons who have entered our armed forces, and I have asked that their names be furnished to me from the files of the War Department. They appear as George A. Walter, Allan J. Walter, Earl S. Walter, Kenneth L. Walter, Stanley S. Walter and Vernon C. Walter, all of the Army.

I can realize the pride which you feel in those fine young men. For my own part, I should like to assure you of the deep appreciation of the nation which has accepted their service with gratitude and a strong sense of responsibility. In the recent anxious months when all our resources were directed to victory over our enemies you have given yours in abundance. I am sure it is a source of deep satisfaction to you, as it is to me, that these boys have played so great a part in the restoration of peace to a troubled world.

Very sincerely yours,

Rbt P. Patterson

Mr. and Mrs. Clark J. Walter
Cinnabar Ranch
Peekskill, New York

The Walter Ranch is a member of the Eastern Dude Ranch Association. The purpose of this organization is to establish and maintain high standards in the Dude Ranch Field. If you vacation at a ranch displaying the EDRA emblem you are assured of the utmost in dude ranching.

A letter received by Mr. Mrs. Walter from the War Department

Timberlane Ranch - 1949
East Jewett, New York

In 1949, after returning from Oklahoma, Tom and Irene Brown moved to Timberlane Ranch in East Jewett, New York. Tom was the corral boss at the ranch. Some of the ranch hands from Cinnabar showed up to work as hands.

ALBANY
WINDHAM
MAPLECREST
HUNTER
TIMBERLANE SKI RANCH
East Jewett
TANNERSVILLE
CATSKILL
HAINESFALL
PALENVILLE
PHOENICIA
SAUGERTIES
WOODSTOCK
KINGSTON
HIGHLAND CIRCLE
MIDDLETOWN
NEWBURGH
TROY
HUDSON
RHINEBECK
POUGHKEEPSIE
BEACON
PEEKSKILL
YONKERS
NEW YORK
N.Y.
MASS.
CONN.
TIMBERLANE
Ski
SUN VALLEY OF THE CATSKILLS
EAST JEWETT N.Y.

PARKER MT. EL. 3574 FT.
2000 ACRES OF VARIED SKI TERRAIN FOR NOVICE, INTERMEDIATE OR EXPERT. 3200 FT. OF TOW LINES
EXTRA SKIING HOURS
TIMBERLANE
East Jewett N.Y.
Ski TRAILS
TOW LINE
SKIERS REST
END of the TRAIL
EXPERT
5 Snortin Run
4 Rip Van Winkle Trail
3 Buckaroo
INTERMEDIATE
2 Deer Run
9 Big Bear Slope
10 Parker Slope
1 Spruce Top
NOVICE
8 Ski School Slope
7 Thriller Slide
6 Rumpus Slope

TIMBERLANE Ski RANCH

New York's Foremost Year Round Playground

Photos: Skating, In the Ice Corral, Novice, Group Around Fireplace, In Corral Room, Under Direction of Allen Seligman, Ski Slope, Ski Lodge

ALL EXPENSE SKI TOURS
Make Your Reservations Now For 2 Day Weekends, 2 Weeks, or Holidays

$23.00 2 DAY ALL EXPENSE TOURS
Includes Meals, Transportation and Instructions
Phone: STillwell 4-0110
MAKE ALL HOLIDAY RESERVATIONS EARLY

SKI LODGE RATES
3 Meals & Lodging
$7.50 and up

RATES IN NEARBY TOURIST HOMES
$2.50 and up

● **WHY YOU'LL LIKE TIMBERLANE**
Only three and one-half hours from New York giving you more skiing hours

● **YOU'LL LIKE EAST JEWETT**
Because of its freshness and wonderful mountain terrain.

● **BECAUSE OF THE HIGH ELEVATION**
We are always blessed with snow from early winter to spring

● **ALL SLOPES AND TRAILS**
Within three hundred yards of the resort

● **FUN IN THE CORRAL ROOM**
If during the day you are tired and prefer to sip a cocktail, hot buttered rum, or have a tasty sandwich by the fireplace, you can always do so in the Corral Room.

● **LONG WINTER EVENINGS**
Are gay around the Pony Bar while you enjoy cocktails and swap tall stories of christies and sitzmarks - where one can also polka round and square dance to music of a fine orchestra.

FOR SNOW REPORTS
Check local Ski Bureau or daily Newspaper - or STillwell 4-0110 in L.I.C.

DIRECTIONS FROM N.Y.C. BY TRAIN
N.Y. Central to Hudson, N. then taxi to Ranch.

BY BUS
Trailways to Tannersville - then Taxi

BY CAR
To Poughkeepsie - cross Bridge to 9-W to Kingston, Saugerties - Rt. 32 to Palenville - Rt. 23A to Tannersville turn up hill at Post Office Stone Church, then bear left Ranch - follow Directional Arrows

"Sun Valley and Golden West of the East." Only 3 ½ Hrs. from N.Y.C. by car, bus or train, and only 50 Min. by plane. Part of the ranch life is the weekly hot dog roast over an open fire, enjoying at the same time your favor tunes sung by the ranch hands.

Timberlane Guest Ranch, East Jewett, Greene County, New York. "Sun Valley and Golden West of the East." Gay couples enjoy Square Dancing and the rhythm of popular music, or sip cocktails at the unique Pony Bar, and listen to their favorite entertainers.

It's restful, it's charming, reaping with fun, sport, gaiety and romance.

A typical scene of a riding group crossing brook on
one of many trails at Timberlane Ranch.

Ad from 1953 Madison Square Garden Rodeo Program

Tom Brown, Jack Ahern, John Rogers, and Jake Kornhaas

Souvenir postcard from
Timberlane Ranch
East Jewitt, New York

- 149 -

Calico Ranch - 1952
Wurtsboro, New York

This ranch just happened. This great property had been used as a retreat for a labor union. It was completely furnished, all separate little cabins, with a lovely large main building for kitchen, dining room, bar, and dance hall. There were great stables, beautiful country, wonderful trails, all ready to go. Tom and Irene just sent out personal letters to their life-long ranch friends and had all the cabins rented for the season. Most of these folks had their own horses, so they were boarded. Earl and Dotty Walter worked there and C.J. and Connie summered there, so there was an experienced crew and family as well. Of course the ladies did the cooking and cleaning, but this was a wonderful life and it was a good operation. Life long friends were made there. The Dabreau family came from the Bronx. They had two young boys who had saved their money from paper routes, and made reservations for two weeks at the ranch that summer. The Dabreau family drove up and left their sons Lenny and Bob with us. Two weeks later, the folks came up for the boys, but the boys hid and didn't come back until late. In the mean time, the Browns asked the folks if the boys could spend the last week of their summer vacation with them. They had become very good help in the barns for Tom, and were really nice boys, so they stayed on, and became adopted kids. Bob married the Brown's daughter Connie, after he served in the U.S. Navy.

Earl, Dottie, their son Earl, Irene and George in front of "Texas", one of the seasonal cottages

Flying W Ranch - 1955
Newtown, Connecticut

This ranch was the last attempt by C.J. Walter to get back into dude ranching. The ranch started out in 1952 as the Ten-C Ranch, owned and operated by ten businessmen from Bridgeport, Connecticut. They called themselves the "10 comedians," - hence the name Ten-C. A lot of money was put into the operations, but there were only a few benefit rodeos. "C.J." was hired in 1955 as manager to make the operation a success. There were extensive renovations, including a swimming pool and living quarters for "C.J." and his wife. Joe Breckenridge joined the ranch as cowboy, horse trainer, and rodeo rider. He also painted murals on the walls and ceilings of the bar, restaurant and snack bar. George Walter was in charge of the horses. "C.J." only enjoyed one year at this ranch, as the ranch was closed due to financial problems.

C.J. Walter and Ranch Hands at Flying W

THE SILVER CITY SAGA

by Daniel Cruson

There is no stranger name for a Newtown road than Silver City Road. This relatively new development road off the norther portion of Hanover Road sounds more like a quaint Colorado thoroughfare than a backwoods Newtown street, but hidden in that name is an almost forgotten episode in recent Newtown history. This road runs along the northern edge of what was once a dude ranch that, between 1952 and 1958, was known successively as the Ten-C and Flying W ranches. In its final incarnation in 1958 it became Silver City, a full scale replica of a fanciful western town complete with Indian village. This "Old Wild West of the East," which was frequently beset by financial and legal problems, lasted only two years, but its story forms one of the more bizarre chapters in the town's history.

The first dude ranch, Ten-C, began as a result of a very successful benefit rodeo for mentally handicapped children which was held on Memorial Day, 1952. Ten Bridgeport business men and western horse enthusiasts came together to stage that rodeo and after it was over they were inspired to create a more permanent facility where future rodeos could be held and people from the area could come for recreation and horseback riding. A series of "bull" sessions were held over the course of the summer and plans were slowly formulated for a dude ranch. Also out of these sessions came the observation by Basil "Duke" Dueschle that, "This is a bunch of comedians." Somehow that comment seemed so appropriate that the enterprise became known and incorporated as Ten-C.

The biggest step forward for this group was to purchase land for their ranch. In the fall of 1952, the large McLaughlin estate on the northern end of Hanover Road became available and the Ten-C corporation purchased 90 acres of it on October 27th. The old McLaughlin house and barn, which would form the center of the dude ranch complex, was located on the west side of Hanover Road about three driveways south of the present Silver City Road. That third driveway was the entrance and is all that is physically left of the ranch today.

The founder's group was led by Louis Lewis who was the head of the Radio Printing Company and would be the one personality who remained with the ranches through their various incarnations. In early October 1952, he characterized the goals of the ranch as follows: "This is not to be a ranch for the elite. It is a place of fun and enjoyment for the entire family—with good horses, good food, good fun and good fellowship."

To reach this goal the group agreed that about $250,000 would be needed to renovate and construct the ranch facilities and this amount was to be raised through the sale of stock in the corporation. Most of that stock was to be held by the principle founders, but shares were to be offered to the public as well at $10.00 each. With this money, the existing house and outbuilding were to be renovated and a series of ranch buildings constructed. Barns were to be built to house 100 horses, of which 50 would be for hire by visitors. The main house would become the "Silver Dollar" Cafe where change would be given in silver dollars. There would also be a silo room for dining, and outside a swimming pool utilizing the fresh water stream, picturesquely called Muddy Brook, that ran through the property. There would also be a rodeo area consisting of a large ring to serve both as an exhibition area and a practice riding area, around which bleachers would be constructed to hold 5,000 people. Another building would be a general store, complete with a cracker barrel and checker board. In addition, there would be a pony ring for youngsters and the stream would be stocked with trout for fishing. Their plans were ambitious and, although several of these features such as the rodeo area and Silver Dollar Cafe would be realized, the complete dream of creating an "Equine Eden" in Newtown would never materialize.

On Sunday, June 14, 1952, the Ten-C ranch was ready to hold its first public event, a "western show" featuring many different classes of competitive races along with performances of trick and fancy riding by Barbara Hart of New York City, sharpshooting by "Diamond Ted" Lewis, one of the world's leading sharpshooters, and trick roping by Jetta, one of the world's youngest performers in the rodeo business. Overall, one hundred riders were expected to come from all over New England and New York State to compete for various prizes.

Riding the colors for the grand entry were two men who were principally responsible for the actual working of the ranch. Serving as barn foreman was Pat "Rags" Mucherino from Fairfield who had been working rodeos in the Northeast for several years and was considered one of the best all-around cowboys in the east and also one of the more successful show organizers. The ranch foreman was Hank Hylen who had already made a reputation for himself locally as a star on that newly emerging electronic device called television. He had been the equestrian marshal of the Barnum Festival for the previous five years, but it was his Master Ranch Club on WNHC-TV that had established him and his palomino horse "Master" as local celebrities. It was hoped this would draw in enough western enthusiasts to put the ranch on a paying basis. The announcement advertising this show, however, noted that the bleachers had not been built yet and that spectators should bring blankets to spread on the hillside overlooking the arena. Even with the roughness of being new and still under construction, the Ten-C's first venture appears to have been a success.

With this event's success, it is strange that there were not more shows of this type. For the rest of the year, the ranch seemed to serve those who wished to hire a horse to ride the extensive trails which now extended across the hill behind the ranch and down as far as Pond Brook. Other trails had been cut with the permission of adjoining landowners through several large areas of open space, so a ranch ride could be lengthened to several miles. The ranch also served as a place to stable one's own horse and

From Newtown History Book – Supplied by Newtown Historical Society

throughout these early years at least ten and as many as 20 horse owners availed themselves of this service.

The ranch also tried to be a good member of the community, although efforts sometimes got out of control. During the summer of 1953, the ranch cooperated with the Newtown Summer Recreation Program to supply riding opportunities for the town's youth at the reduced rate of $1.00 per morning per rider. The first morning of the riding program, 30 youngsters showed up at the ranch to the consternation of Hank Hylen since the ranch only had ten horses for hire. A weekly schedule was quickly set up which distributed the rider load over three days and the program was off and running toward a successful first season. The few available horses, however, indicates that the ranch was hardly running at full capacity, presaging future troubles.

The second year of operation was marked by a similar summer recreation program and with a slowly growing numbers of weekend riders coming from New Haven, New York and the shore towns to enjoy a horse ride through the wild and natural beauty that characterized northern Newtown in the 1950s. Toward the end of their active season, another "western show," or rodeo as it was now called, was held with stars coming from all over the northeast and even a few that were on the rodeo circuit from the real west. This show was billed as Pat Mucherino's last appearance in the east. He was leaving the ranch to pursue riding fortunes in the authentic west of Arizona. Hank Hyland remained as the chief manager of the ranch.

The beginning of the 1955 season saw some substantial changes made. It is not clear whether these changes were a result of financial difficulties which would plague the operation in later years, or whether there was simply a desire to reorganize into a more efficient business. In December of 1954, the operation is sold to Hanover Hills Inc., a holding company consisting of substantially the same directors as the old Ten-C. The name of the ranch was changed to the Flying W and a $100,000 expansion planned. This money was to be raised through stock sales which suggests that the old owners were interested in diversifying the financial risk of operating the ranch. Publicly they claimed that they wanted to turn the ranch into a "money-making enterprise," which apparently the old ranch had not been.

The key to the new ranch's success was to be C.J. Walter who took over as ranch manager in February 1955. C.J. was a real cowboy. For the previous 30 years he had been in the ranch managing business and over half of that time was spent successfully managing dude ranches in the east including the Cimarron and Cinnabar Ranches, both in Peekskill, and the Lost Wilderness in New Boston, MA. He had also helped Buster Crabbe get his ranch started in New Jersey. In addition, he was one of the founders of the Dude Ranch Association which boasted such prestigious members as Roy Rogers and Gene Autry.

His background was more deeply rooted in the west than simply managing dude ranches, however. He was born in Saskatchewan, Canada where his ranching career began with herding cattle at age 16. His father, Loan Walter, who was still alive at 94 in 1955, was one of the few remaining Indian Fighters. During his youth he had known Chiefs Sitting Bull, Crazy Horse and Rain In The Face, and had fought against the Sioux in the Battle of Wounded Knee.

Most of his stories, however, were of his own experiences with outlaws such as the Anderson brothers:

"They were horse thieves and Gus was their leader. Out in Montana one night, they crossed our path and asked us to feed them. We gave them some grub and bedded down almost 30 feet away, but we couldn't sleep a wink all night because we was afraid they'd steal our stock... Kept my gun handy right by my side. I had two young Norwegian boys with me, but they weren't much good. Scared to death they was... The law finally caught up with the Andersons at Big Butte, took 'em to Bismark, North Dakota for trial and they did seven years for stealing horses.

"Funny thing. I had a chance to talk with Gus many years later. He laughed about the night we gave him the grub. Said he didn't sleep a wink either. Thought we were going to steal his horses..."

C.J. came to Newtown with a considerable family of six boys and four girls, all of whom had acted with him in Western movies or as he put it, "...few great Western movies have been made the past several decades in which he or his children or grandchildren did not cavort in front of the camera." The last film in which he himself appeared was "High Noon" with Gary Cooper. He had also been associated with Tom Mix in the rodeo business in Montana in 1926. With credentials like this, it would seem that the success of the Flying W would be assured even if people only patronized the place to hear the stories of this Western movie relic.

To further insure their success, there were extensive renovations to the facilities, especially to the Silver Dollar. It was enlarged so the restaurant could accommodate 60 people and the tavern area was equipped with a 30 foot mahogany bar. In addition, a lodge/motel was to be built. This new lodge was to be constructed of white cedar logs with large overhanging eaves and be large enough to house 60 guests in ten deluxe double rooms and two dormitory wings which would accommodate another 20 guests each. This C-shaped building was to be 365 feet long and contain a ranch office in its center section along with a spacious foyer and living quarters for Mr. Walter. Along with this, a swimming pool was finally put in and a huge new barn that could house 60 horses was constructed.

In that same year, 1955, another character was added to the payroll who served to draw curious locals into the Silver Dollar. Joseph Breckenridge came to the Flying W as a cowboy, horse trainer and rodeo rider, but what made him unique was his reputation as the world's fastest painter. His work adorned the walls and ceiling of the Silver Dollar bar, restaurant, and snack bar and he so impressed local customers with his demonstrations that many commissioned him to paint murals in their play rooms. He had taught himself to paint 48 years before and still mixed his own colors from herbs, flowers and roots, techniques that he had supposedly picked up from the

Sioux Indians living in Fort Peck, Montana. According to observers, he could paint a mural measuring four by eight feet in less than one minute. His painting methods occasionally employed a frying pan for a brush, but his favorite tool was a house painting brush measuring six inches wide. With this he painted the walls of the Silver Dollar with buffalo herds, pack horses in the snow, lone bull elk, mountain sheep, Indian scenes and birds on the wing, all of which reportedly drew great praise from visitors.

Even as the renovations were being brought to completion, trouble was brewing in the form of a disgruntled contractor who had not been paid. On March 29, 1955, G and J Builders place an attachment on both Hanover Hills Inc. and the Flying W for the amount of $2,000, and for the next year the ranch seemed to be under a financial cloud. By June of 1956, the extent of their financial troubles becomes public knowledge when a Bridgeport judge appointed two temporary co-receivers to devise a plan to reorganize the corporation which would benefit both the stockholders and creditors. On January 17, 1956 they became permanent. According to a statement made by Mr. Harold Dow, the president and chairman of the board, other stock holders had lost interest in the venture and it was threatened with bankruptcy as creditors began demanding immediate payment of their claims.

The receivers took over a year before they were ready to arrange for the disposition of the property and its buildings. A public sale was scheduled for December 16, 1957, but before that sale could take place it was discovered that the deed which transferred the property from the old Ten-C corporation to Hanover Hills was invalid because there had never been a Hanover Hills Corporation. A court order was needed to reform the original deed so that the property was transferred to Newtown Associates Incorporated, a land holding company which had been incorporated in 1954 to, "...buy, own, sell, and exchange real estate and to conduct and carry on a summer and winter resort..." This wrinkle apparently delayed the sale and it was not until April 9, 1958 that the property was finally sold for $29,000.

The buyer of the now defunct ranch was Louis Lewis who had been one of the principal incorporators of the original Ten-C. Within a month, it became apparent that he had plans for rehabilitating the ranch, turning it into a wild west ranch called Silver City Ranch. This was to be no simple dude ranch, however, but rather a western town complete with wild Indians, outlaws, a marshal and a full compliment of western events.

The grand opening was a month after the purchase, in May of 1958. The ads of the time called it "The Old Wild West of the East," and claimed that it was, "... a children's Mecca, a paradise for would-be Lone Rangers, Wild Bill Hickocks, Matt Dillons, Roy Rogerses, etc. They revel in being appointed deputy to Silver City's Marshal Butler. They glory in meeting Chief White Cloud and his band of Sioux braves. They thrill to see Frank Dalton's "gang" rob the town bank and the battle of O.K. Corral, trick riding by "Daredevil" Fran Crethers, and fancy sharpshooting and archery." In addition, visiting children would thrill to ride on the Silver City stagecoach, horses, surreys and jeep train while parents would enjoy "wandering through an exact replica of a typical frontier town with its gun shop, Wells Fargo station, livery stable, trading post, marshal's office, blacksmith shop, and jail." In a clearing in the woods, just a short distance from the town replica, was an Indian village, "with real Pawnee Indians from Oklahoma." All of this could be enjoyed for a mere 75¢ for adults and 50¢ for children.

Silver City's first year seemed to be a real success. When they opened for the second year in May 1959, they advertised that the parking facilities had been greatly expanded to overcome the road congestion on Hanover Road that had plagued the previous year. The Board of Selectmen also seemed to appreciate the ranch's success and with alacrity they extended a special permit to allow the opening show of the season to on a Sunday. A steady stream of ads were placed in *The Bee* announcing special activities and shows right through the fall of 1959, indicating that the ranch was enjoying a vigorous season.

That summer, Richard Belval was Frank Dalton. He had replaced a friend who had played the part during the previous summer and, in a recent interview, he explained how much fun being a frontier outlaw in Newtown could be. He had been taking karate for some time and knew how to fall. As a result, he was designated to fire on the respectable townsmen from the roof of one of the buildings. At a climactic moment, he would be shot and fall onto the roof of the addition and from there to the ground. He claims that this was a real crowd pleaser.

An even greater crowd pleaser was being hanged every Sunday. He would be captured and incarcerated in the town jail. Before long, a lynch mob would work itself up to taking the law into its own hands and head to the jail with a rope. After breaking him out of jail, they took him to a tree up on the hill and hanged him. He was actually trussed up in a parachute harness which was concealed under his baggy clothes and the harness was attached to the rope after the noose was placed around his neck. One afternoon the harness began to slip and the noose tightened. Since he had his hands tied behind his back there were a few anxious moments before he was freed from impending disaster. After that he just held his hands behind his back. As he summed it up, "We did it all for the kids!"

Belval also observed that the ersatz western town attracted great crowds throughout the summer. Then, very mysteriously the advertisements cease. In all of 1960 there are no ads, not even a news article announcing a show or special event. All of the town records are silent and Silver City is not even mentioned in the land or court records. Belval remembered that there were rumors of several owners who were skimming money from the operation, so it was probably mismanagement rather than lack of public interest that did in Newtown's premier weekend attraction.

The ranch may have operated in a limited fashion and for a short period of time as a dude ranch after 1960, but the Silver City Bar and Restaurant seems to have continued operation with its reputation becoming increasingly seedy as the decade progressed. Several local residents remember that strange couples could be seen on weekends in some of the building on the property and accusations of immoral conduct were rife. The bar appeared to be the centerpiece in arranging these illegal trysts.

By the late 1960s, the Western Village, Indian settlement and horse barns had been clearly abandoned. The last mention of Silver City in the local newspapers was in 1972. On Monday, September 11th, a fire of suspicious origins broke out and completely destroyed the main building. This had housed the old restaurant and had originally been the McLaughlin homestead. Meanwhile, foreclosure proceeding were being held which would transfer the property and its remaining buildings to the Hartford National Bank by the end of that month. Again, the fire engines were called out to vainly try to save the main horse barn in October. All is quiet for the next five years. In July of 1977, the Hartford National Bank sold the property to local developer Clifford O'Dell, and the present housing development is born. In an ironic twist, the name of the ill-fated ranch survives in the name of the access road to that development, Silver City Road, and the new residents on that street must wonder about its most un-New England name.

★

Estelle Gilbert tending bar at the Flying W

C.J. watching the ride getting ready to head out

Westbury Sunday Republican - 1955

C. J. AND SON GEORGE talk over plans for the Flying "W" up in Newtown. When it opens early in July it will, C. J. says, be one of the finest dude ranches in the East.—Goodman Photos.

Westbury Sunday Republican – March 6, 1955

Touch of Old West in Newtown as C.J. Walter goes Ranching There

Colorful figure of Rodeos, Dude Ranches, Western Scenes has Wealth of Experience; 94 Year-Old Father great story teller; Cowboy Art Predominates

By John DiCorpo

It was a raw day, damp and cold. An anemic February sun gave light but no warmth to the craggy New England landscape in a woody, hill-and dale part of Newtown. We hiked up a muddy trail to a large, rambling building advertised as the Silver Dollar Bar and Restaurant. We stepped into the place and plumb into a replica of the Old West. Murals on the wall, all authentic scenes of the old days when the covered wagons ambled through dense wilderness and the pioneers hacked out ranches and small towns where law and order were unknown; a huge mahogany bar, a couple of wagon-wheels doubling as light fixtures hung from the ceiling; but what attracted the eye were the men working about in Western garb.

C.J. Walter was bossing the goings-on, the start of what is to be the biggest and best dude ranch in the East, or at least so he says. If money talks, then $350,000 (honest, that's what he told us!) is going to be spent to achieve this distinction for the Flying "W." That, podner, is a fair passel of dinero to be spent on the 400 acre spread with its 40 miles of trails. It is scheduled to open July 1.

C.J. is leaving the first of next month to buy his "hosses" in Ardmore and Ada, Oklahoma; he is passing the word among his staff of 22 to make plans to come to work. The architect is all finished with the blueprints for the main lodge which will sleep 75 and the dining room which will accommodate more than that number. The new barn will house about 60 horses; there'll be enough room for 22 boarders. Enough statistics.

Stumping around in there round-heeled Western boots, with their cuffs stuffed in, checkered shirts open at the neck, all wearing 10-gallon hats, were a few of C.J.'s friends and one of his boys, George; a long, lean, lithe cowboy who holds a few riding and roping records around the country, having taken part in rodeos from Mexico to Canada, not to mention Cuba. C.J. and his missus have been blessed with a fine family, everyone a crack rider and finished ranch hand. Six boys and four girls, we'll give you a rundown on them later, bear the Walter's brand.

He's Been Around

Sitting down chewing the fat at the Silver Dollar bar (no liquor yet, no license) the circle of talkers grew bigger. C.J. held the floor, he's the venerable one. Ranching at the age of 16 with his Dad, who is still alive and a spry 94, (he'll be at the ranch this summer and can tell you some Indian stories that'll curl your hair). C.J. rode herd up Saskatchewan way, became a Canadian subject to become eligible for free range. He stayed three decades, decided to come back, hurried across the line and regained his coveted U.S. citizenship, then went into dude ranching. He has been in it for the past 18 years, started the famous Cimarron ranch spread in Peekskill, N.Y., with his brother Vern, then his own Cinnabar, both of which received elaborate spreads in Colliers, The Saturday Evening Post, and other magazines.

We had an interesting hour, listening to C.J. spin his tales of the Old West, stories of the bad men, outlaws, horse thieves, some of whom he know intimately, respected 'em, too. Why? Well, he tells of Long George, last name Francis but few knew it, one of the best shots in the West. Who was going to argue who could do things with a six shooter this big string bean could do.

"Long George used to operate in the Harver, Montana area. Used to fan out to the Bear Paw mountains in his journeyin' around. He was tall as a tree, could shoot snowbirds, you people call 'em sparrows around here, right out of the air with his .44. Form the hip, too," C.J. Shakes his head in obvious admiration.

"For practice we used to throw a tomato can up in the air and bet who could keep it up there the longest shootin' at it. But these outlaws were rugged, dead shots. Most of the time they would hang around Minot, North Dakota where nobody would bother them. They never pulled off anything in that town so the sheriff let them alone. Long George finally got caught, a sheriff got the drop on him. Was up in Highland, Montana, he brought him in, Long George stood trial, got 10 years at Deer Lodge, but he never served it. He managed to get a hold of a gun, backed right out of the courtroom; nobody dared take a shot at him, and beat it. Then he openly appeared in different places, but he was too smart to get cornered. Funny thing how he died. Took a shine to a school teacher, drove up with a car loaded with a couple boxes of apples for the kids in her class; he hit something in the road and the car turned over. The bone in his leg came through the flesh, he tried to crawl to a homesteaders' place two miles away, never made it, got within a half mile of it, though, then shot himself, that's how they found him. There were 600 at the funeral, including ranchers, cowboys, and a lot of sheriffs. They respected him," C.J. averred.

Bronco Buster

Born on a ranch near Standing Rock Reservation, South Dakota. C.J. came from a family of three boys and four girls, was an expert cowpuncher and broke horses when just a kid. His dad owned the Lone "L" in south Dakota, near the Sioux reservation, and C.J. learned to speak the language fluently.

When he was a young man he traveled with the herds up to the Saskatchewan territory, saw the vast vacant country, not even surveyed, no railroad, but he saw possibilities in it. He took the first ranch property in sight on Broken Shell Creek, he was about 17 at the time, but when the railroad came through he pushed further West, 90 miles or so.

If a man didn't have free range he just couldn't afford to ranch. That was the fact, plain and simple, C.J. said, and he bitterly assailed the homesteaders, "those sod-busters" who migrated in quickly from the Dakotas, Ohio, Minnesota in the early 1900's.

"They just spoiled it for the ranchers. They put in a crop of wheat in their half sections which wouldn't grow, the soil isn't right for it, you know. Grain just won't come up if its so dry. The history of the Montana's, the Dakota's, and the Saskatchewan proves it, just too blamed dry, its part of the great American desert. Dust and grasshoppers gave us fits around the 1930's – raised hell all through the territory," he said.

"Today?" we urged gently. "Well," he answered, "there is irrigation and better farming methods that partly licked the problem, but they still don't belong," C.J. grumbled adamantly.

C.J. went back a bit to his description of the outlaw country 40 years ago. "It was pretty wild up there then. Horse thieves were around all the time. I remember one bunch, the Anderson brothers, Gus was the leader. They came by one night and asked us to feed them. We gave them some supper, bedded down about 30 feet from them, didn't sleep a wink all night, was afraid they'd steal our stock. Kept my gun handy right by my side. I had two young Norwegian boys with me, they weren't much good, scared to death they was," C.J. grinned.

Real Rustlers

"They finally caught up with the Anderson brothers in Big Butte, took 'em to Bismarck, North Dakota for trial, they did seven years for stealing horses. They'd take a herd to Canada, sell 'em, get another bunch there and take those back to Nebraska, the Dakotas, Montana and sell them.

"Funny thing, I had a chance to talk to Gus many years later. He laughed about that night we gave his crew some grub. Said he didn't get a wink of sleep that night either, thought we were going to steal his horses," he said.

C.J. got itchy after 30 years in Canada, got himself in the rodeo circuit, toured the West with his C.J. Ranch Rodeo Show, then brought the whole shooting match East, touring all the principal cities. This prepared him for the dude ranch business; he left Cimarron up in Peekskill to start Cinnabar, had that for seven years, but it fell prey to a housing project and C.J. accepted the Flying "W" project with alacrity. "Gonna have a modern arena here, seating over 2000, have a rodeo every Sunday for the summer. We'll have guest appearances from some of the best in the business, but anyone staying here can take part. We're going to train 'em, we'll teach riding, roping and all the cowboy sports," he glowed. "And we'll have overnight trips, right near some good water, the guests will eat and sleep out, they'll love it," he said, adding, "our hosses will be trained and gentle for those who want them that way."

C.J. says that three-quarter of his guests come from the New York area, about 20 percent from Boston. That's the way it was up in the Cinnabar dude ranch.

Aside from C.J.'s father, who, as we mentioned, is 94, who divides his time between C.J. and Vern, there are 10 kids in the family. C.J. hailed George to help think up the married names of the boys and girls. The list goes like this: Vern, who lives in Waterbury, "married an eastern girl, she took him away from ranching," C.J. said with a glint in his eye; Allan, who owns a tavern in Staatsburg, NY; Stanley, a resident of Tucson, Arizona, who ranches and loves it out there; Kenneth, General Foods employee of White Plains, NY, "he's a real smart boy that one," C.J. opines; Earl, now in Kissimmee, Florida, married a trick riding gal, both rodeo performers, and both whom will be at the Flying "W;" George, already in Newtown at the Flying "W," who will be corral boss, a first class rodeo performer, Connecticut's champion bronco buster; then there's four girls, Mrs. Jose Ferrante of Northern Holliwood, California, both she and her husband are in the movies, but there 12 year old son is already serving notice he's going to outshine them as he has been featured in "The Mark of the Scorpion," Mrs. Tom Brown of Laurens, New York, married to a horse dealer; Mrs. Bill Schwerd, Harwick, NY whose husband is a trick rider and rodeo performer, and Mrs. Red Sloan, New Canaan, where Red runs a riding school. "Had 'em all with me at Cinnabar but when the ranch closed down they all drifted away, now I don't think I'll get too many of them back," C.J. said mournfully, adding "they're all damn good rodeo performers."

Great Artist

The conversation broadened to take in a couple of fellows that had been kibitzing all the time. One was Joe Breckenridge, C.J. says of him "he's the most outstanding cowboy artist in the world. Appeared in the first issue of Life, never had a lesson in his life and has been painting from coast to coast. Joe and I became good friends up at a Saskatchewan rodeo. He got pretty badly hurt up there, got dragged around some. Gassed and wounded in the first World War, too. But he's a great guy to have around," he continued, glancing fondly at Joe. The latter has quietly cut up a piece of beaver board, armed himself with a two and four inch paint brush, poured out half a dozen small portions of house paint and in less than 10 minutes painted the most beautiful landscape you ever saw.

Bill Vogel, who used to take the part of Buffalo Bill in C.J.'s traveling Western show, and later became special effects director at CBS, has had a long and honorable career with the movies, the leading movie, radio and TV performers among his friends, chimed in with quite a few interesting anecdotes.

"Think these fellows can tell a story. Come up this summer and hear my Dad tell about the Indian days," C.J. invited.

C.J. is manager and a stockholder in the Flying "W" and the rest of the stock is owned by a group of Bridgeport businessmen. ~

Lost Wilderness Ranch - 1953

New Boston, Massachusetts

This was another ranch that C.J. and some of the family managed in Massachusetts. C.J. held rodeos and managed the ranch with the usual Walter charm. It is at this ranch that C.J. and Connie met John F. Kennedy when he was running for the Senate.

C.J., Connie, Ken, Barbara Walter and their boys at the Lost Wilderness dining room.

Lost Wilderness trail ride.

Ad from 1953 Madison Square Garden Rodeo Program

AuSable Guest Ranch
1953 - 1954
Gaylord, Michigan

OLD WEST MOVES INTO AU SABLE

C. J. WALTER and his Horse NAVAJO

Main Building

New Manager Brings Spirit of Old West to AuSable Ranch

"Cowboy's Cowboy" — that's C. J. Walter, Manager of the 9000 Acre Au Sable Guest Ranch near Gaylord, Michigan.

GAYLORD, MICH.—Walter has a special way of describing the Au Sable, which offers guests riding every day, with the largest string of Western horses in Michigan. "We call this the ranchiest ranch east of Wyoming," says C. J., and he ought to know.

For C. J. Walter is a true son of the old West. Born and raised on a ranch near Standing Rock Reservation, South Dakota, he started breaking horses and cowpunching at an early age, and took part in his first rodeo show when only 16.

In addition to his authentic western background, Walter is an experienced dude ranch operator. He opened and for many years he managed the famous Cimmaron and Cinnabar Ranches in New York State — widely renowned throughout the country, having been pictured and described in such magazines as the Saturday Evening Post, Colliers, and metropolitan newspapers.

Walter's principal aim at the Au Sable Guest Ranch is to offer his guests "the real thing" in the way of Western hospitality. Nothing is spared at Au Sable to make the guest feel right at home; to help guests build true and lasting friendships, and to provide the utmost in the way of fun and sport.

In his youth, Walter trailed in a covered wagon to the Saskatchewan territory, settling for a while north of Montana. These were the years when outlaws still hid out in the wild country, and "C.J." knew many of them—the Anderson Boys, Dutch Henry, and Long George, among others. Later he joined a wild west show touring the western states, eventually going east where his C.J. Ranch Rodeo Show played in all the principal cities.

Walter's family of six boys and four girls have carried on the family tradition—all are active ranchers or rodeo contest riders. Along with cowboys from Texas, Arizona, and Montana, they guide Au Sable guests through the many and varied activities that make a stay at the ranch such a memorable occasion. Riding the trails through the scenic wonders of northern Michigan during the day, singing their songs and telling tales of the old West 'round the evening campfire, square dancing, boating, swimming —these are a few of the many activities. To give Au Sable guests something to remember their vacation by, the Ranch operates a Western store, where souvenirs and novelties, as well as Levis, boots, spurs, and "10-gallon" hats may be bought.

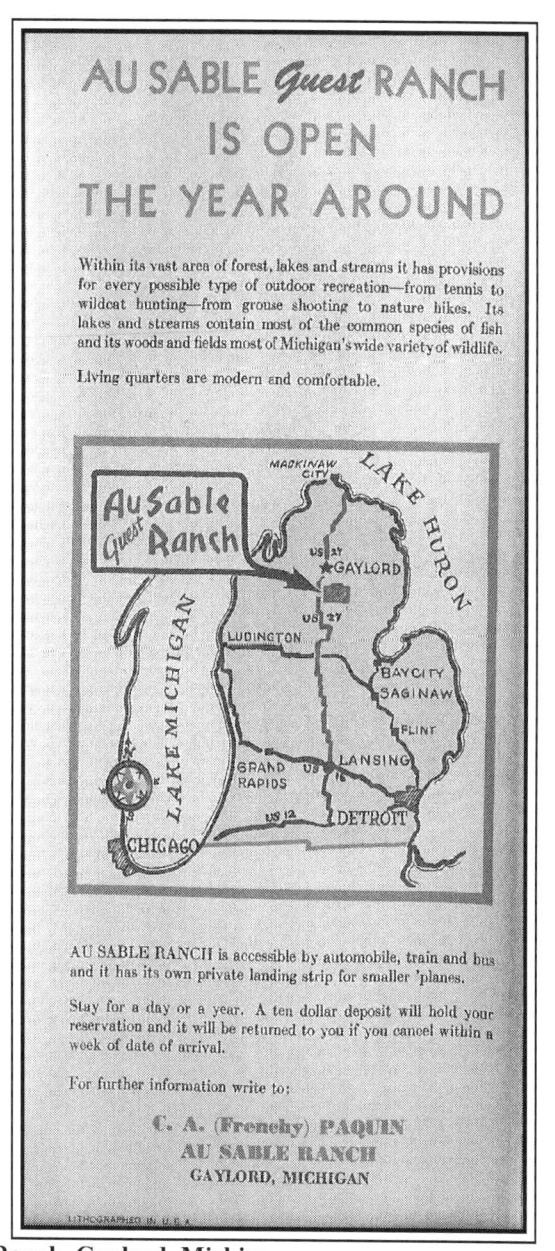

Brochure of AuSable Guest Ranch, Gaylord, Michigan

- 164 -

EVERYTHING OUTDOOR MICHIGAN HAS TO OFFER
On the Top of

MICHIGAN in Oscoda County, five miles south of Gaylord and 22 miles north of Grayling, lies the 9,000-acre domain of AUSABLE RANCH. Two miles east of Highway US-27, reached by a well signed road, is the Ranch headquarters with its beautiful and spacious guest lodge accommodating more than 100 persons.

For Miles in every direction radiate trails leading through hunting grounds and to lakes and streams—all available for the free use of AU SABLE RANCH guests. There is something interesting to see or do every week of the year. In the Winter there are skiing, snowshoeing, ice fishing, fox, rabbit and bobcat hunting, and just plain enjoyment of the white fresh snow in invigorating air. In the Spring there are hikes through the acres of wildflowers and there is fishing for rainbow, brown and brook trout. Summer at AU SABLE brings riding through 80 miles of woodland trails; fishing in the 20 private lakes; swimming in isolated beaches; driving along shaded roads to watch deer and other wildlife; loafing on the long lodge portico; and all the other things that go to make a pleasant and interesting vacation. Then the Fall brings the grouse and duck hunters; those who leave the brilliant colors of the northern hardwood forests; the archers and then, in late November, the red-clad deer hunters.

ALL these things . . .
ARE YOURS TO ENJOY IF YOU ARE A GUEST AT AU SABLE RANCH!!!

- 166 -

GUESTS!
...URS TO ENJOY

RELAX UNDISTURBED

FOR ALL THE FAMILY

AU SABLE is ideal. There is a playground for the children, and a concrete tennis court. Beaches are safe. Mother and the children may pick wild berries in season. Arrangements may be made for family picnics. No need for mother to worry about her hair-do nor for Dad to have to change from his fishing or hunting clothes to enter the dining room. Rooms may be arranged for family use.

Trains and busses will be met. Note the arrival time on your reservation card.

Competent hunting and fishing guides are furnished guests.

...our experience. Incidentally, stable charges are the only "extra" at AU SABLE.

...VATIONS WRITE TO:

...y: PAQUIN
...est RANCH
MICHIGAN
Telegraph: Gaylord
Railroad: Michigan Central R.R.

- 167 -

EVERYTHING OUTDOOR MICHIGAN HAS TO OFFER
On the Top of

MICHIGAN in Oscoda County, five miles south of Gaylord and 22 miles north of Grayling, lies the 9,000-acre domain of AU SABLE RANCH. Two miles east of Highway U.S.-27, reached by a well signed road, is the Ranch headquarters with its beautiful and spacious guest lodge accommodating more than 100 persons.

For Miles in every direction radiate trails leading through hunting grounds and to lakes and streams—all available for the free use of AU SABLE RANCH guests. There is something interesting to see or do every week of the year. In the Winter there are skiing, snowshoeing, ice fishing, fox, rabbit and bobcat hunting, and just plain enjoyment of the white fresh snow in invigorating air. In the Spring there are hikes through the acres of wildflowers and there is fishing for rainbow, brown and brook trout. Summer at AU SABLE brings fishing in the 20 private lakes, swimming on isolated beaches, driving along shaded roads to watch deer and other wildlife; loafing on the long lodge portico, and all the other things that go to make a pleasant and interesting vacation. Then the Fall brings the grouse and duck hunters; those who love the brilliant colors of the northern hardwood forests; the archers and then, in late November, the red-clad deer hunters.

ALL these things....
ARE YOURS TO ENJOY IF YOU ARE A GUEST AT AU SABLE RANCH!!!

You Will Be Relaxing
ON TOP OF MICHIGAN
at
Au Sable Ranch

The Ranch is located in the famous Gaylord Hills, the highest point in the southern peninsula of Michigan. Here the air is crisp and fresh. Summers are mild and invigorating. Being in the "snow belt" the winter climate is dry and healthful.

We'll meet you half way at AU SABLE RANCH. Through the north boundary of the Ranch runs the 45th degree of latitude—we are actually just half way between the North Pole and the Equator.

These are but two of the features that make AU SABLE RANCH unique. Its 9,000 acres of hardwoods, pines and cedars are in the very heart of Michigan's grouse and deer country. Its twenty lakes and miles of streams offer bass, trout, perch, pike and other fishing. Its forty miles of trails tempt the rider. Its woods and fields are a source of joy to the nature lover—to mention only a few of the diversified attractions and appeals of AU SABLE.

There is place aplenty for lazy days or energetic activity to suit the inclination of the guest and there is entertainment, too, to pass the evenings, with movies, square dances, beach suppers and such.

Life at AU SABLE is informal. Bring the kind of clothes that will make you comfortable.

SPRING—
SUMMER—
AUTUMN—
WINTER—

ENJOY THEM ALL AT AU SABLE!!!

C.J. Ranch Rodeo

George, C.J., and Stan Walter
During the years, C.J. took his
Rodeo on the road, bringing his
family and horses with him.

C.J. Walter in Navajo

Brochures,

Newsletters,

Memorabilia

From

Cimarron Ranch

And

Cinnabar Ranch

CIMARRON MAIL POUCH

CIMARRON RANCH   FALL 1950   PUTNAM VALLEY, N.Y.

RODEO REUNION OCT. 18

Each year — for eleven years — Cimarron has held a Party — for you! 1950 marks our TWELFTH Annual Party. All your ranch friends will be mighty sad if YOU are not among those present! Check the date on your engagement calendar — don't miss the EVENT OF THE YEAR!!

WHEN?   Wednesday, October 18th. Party starts 5 P.M. Ends ? ?

WHERE?   Hotel Capitol Carnival Room — 50th Street and Eighth Ave., New York City — directly opposite Madison Square Garden.

HOW?   Mail your check or money order FOR $5.00 for EACH RESERVATION to Cimarron Ranch, Putnam Valley, New York, PROMPTLY. Our Madison Square Garden connections have enabled us to guarantee our guests — a solid block of choice SIDE ARENA SEATS — even though public box office demand for selected tickets for the final week of the World's Championship Rodeo are at a premium! Sit with your friends — in a reserved section! PICK UP YOUR RODEO AND REUNION TICKETS AT THE HOTEL CAPITOL CARNIVAL ROOM FROM 5 TO 8:30 P.M. ON THE NIGHT OF THE PARTY.   Dress: — As you please.

WHY?   Because — of rising costs — we have eliminated the Banquet — here is what your $5.00 covers:

PRE-RODEO GET-TOGETHER AT HOTEL CAPITOL COCKTAIL LOUNGE. PARTY SOUVENIR.

WORLDS' CHAMPIONSHIP RODEO SHOW — in the final, most exciting week at Madison Square Garden.

REUNION with your friends at Mike Hastings' Birthday Celebration after the big show.

SQUARE DANCING to Cimarron's Own Square Dance Band in the Hotel Capitol Carnival Room.

And — Because It Won't Be a Party Without You! Don't hear about the Rodeo Reunion Round-Up from Somebody else — we sincerely want YOU to be with us —

                                                                                               Cordially,

VERN   LU   MIKE   BETTY   JIMMY

CIMARRON MAIL POUCH

"WESTERNTOWN WHISPERS"

DO YOU KNOW that...

Cimarron Ranch has a NEW post office address? It's PUTNAM VALLEY, NEW YORK. The Ranch has not moved. We are still in the same lovely valley location. Only one hour from New York City — by fast, dependable New York Central Railroad to Peekskill Station. You will be met by station wagon on advance notification. Or — drive your car — only 50 miles — on fast, connecting parkways.

Cimarron Ranch has a NEW dial telephone number? LAKELAND 8-8003.

Cimarron Ranch has built — for your comfort and enjoyment — a beautiful, *outdoor* dance pavilion — adjoining our Westerntown Powder River Hotel dance floor?

We maintain our own — and exclusive — D.D.T. program? Which, simply stated, means you need not be annoyed by insects, flies or bugs?

Cimarron has a really spacious, natural swimming pool — tennis court — archery range — and guns for target practice?

Our horses are the FINEST that money and "know-how" can provide for your riding enjoyment? Please excuse our pardonable pride on this particular phase of the ranch. Mike Hastings, our barn foreman, is without equal!

Despite rising prices and growing shortages, somehow, Lu and Cimarron's chef, Bill Gallick, still manage to provide plentiful, varied and appetizing menus?

Other than the amount you voluntarily spend, YOU HAVE NO EXTRAS AT CIMARRON? Your hour-by-hour entertainment is INCLUDED in the rate you select. We've spent twelve years perfecting, through experience, MORE FUN AND DIVERSION THAN YOU ACTUALLY HAVE TIME TO ENJOY!

"MAIN STREET" Westerntown

CIMARRON'S CORRAL BOSS

MIKE HASTINGS

JUST BETWEEN OURSELVES...

As we go into our twelfth Fall Season, we're very glad to report that our happy family — guests, management and staff — has maintained old friendships, and acquired *many* new ones. Through our 1950 year, Cimarron's reservation requests have often more than exceeded our accommodation space. Aside from the fact that we sincerely strive to please — perhaps this is due to a realization that outdoor exercise and healthy fun is the necessary antidote to a tension-filled world at war. It is heart-warming to us to know that when our guests come once — they come again — there's a real friendly bond here at Cimarron — Consequently — you'll be interested in knowing that...

"GINNY" (Virginia Baigas) has been chosen to carry our Ranch colors in the Eastern Rodeo Queen Contest, held prior to opening of Madison Square Garden Rodeo. Pretty nice to be photogenic — and a swell gal besides!

"BILL" Gallick — our tried and true Chef since 1944 dashes back from West Palm Beach each Spring — no wonder the meal gong is eagerly waited for!

"CHRIS" is still with us — she heads out Arizona way every winter to make as many friends as she has right here!

"KAY" tiny as she is, totes those big trays — and furthermore — rides a mean quadrille!

"JUNIE" Boyhan — and his bride, "Pat" Mooney are ranching in Wyoming now!

"CAROL" Fulton — is engaged (we hear) to an Army man! Congratulations, Carol!

"SUE" Waitelis — our glamorous Trick-Rider is thrilling our rodeo spectators again. Sue suffered a badly fractured wrist last July. Meanwhile, she's been office assistant — arena rodeo secretary — and a joy to have around!

"FRANK" and "BETTY" Garramone — besides being happily married — have a lovely new home on Canopus Valley Road — nice things should continue to happen to two wonderful people!

"BILLY" Butler — who rides and clowns with the best of of them is now stock farming in Washington, New Jersey — we miss you, Bill, and wish you luck!

"LEE" Wilms — is back with us after wintering way out West. Fully recovered from a near fatal auto accident.

"DICK" Borden — our genial M. C. keeps very busy seeing to it that our guests all have a good time — in addition to announcing our rodeo shows.

"MIKE" Hastings — our "Old Reliable" barn boss keeps everything in A-1 condtion — ably assisted by RICHIE - STAN - ZIP and our other young cowboys!

"OLLIE" Flanner — our Westerntown Snack Bar hostess is responsible for all those clever drawings. Her artistic talents match her many friendships!

"HARRY" Tompkins — carrying the Cimarron banner was 1948 and 1949 World's Champion Bull Rider. Harry rode to the Top in a hurry — married Rosemary Colburn, daughter of the famous rodeo producer — and they are now living in Dublin, Texas!

"SYLVIA" Noel — has efficiently managed, since 1946 — our Silver Saddle Trading Post. Only because we have Sylvia can you get novelties - jeans - or jewelry!

"DAD" Walter — Vern's Dad - beloved by everyone — is going into his ninetieth year! His remarkable alertness and zest for living is a wonderful example for us all!

"JANE" Noordzy — Cimarron's 1949 Rodeo Queen is a married lady now. Just as friendly — just as pretty — our best to you, Jane.

"RAY" Civerchia — Fate smiled on Cimarron way back in 1946 when Ray first became a member of our family. His radiant personality is not confined to our Last Chance Bar — it's all over the ranch!

"JIM" and "PEGGY" Eichler — came over with their handsome little Jimmy, Jr. Big Jim does his usual fine "pick-up" job in our rodeo — his horse, "Expense" is now at Cimarron.

RODEO GAMES

"MARK" and "NENA" Barker — were not with us this year — Mark, along with his other interests, is busy building a political career, out in Mesa, Arizona.

"BOB" and "MARY" Kamps and their five sons have been in Tokyo, Japan, for some time now — Bob is in the U. S. Army Air Corps.

"GEE-GEE" Calcott — and her sturdy four-year old, Jerry, Jr., visited us recently — from San Antonio, Texas!

"MARK" Lewis — Cimarron's official photgrapher has been doing a wonderful job for our guests all this season!

"JOE" Phillips — and his wonder horse "Smokey" has been a high spot of our Sunday Rodeos all season. We've had the pleasure of having Joe with us when he's not showing his marvelous act all over the country. A fine young man has beautifully trained a fine trick horse.

"TEX" Foster — makes the arena crowd look on with envy when he twirls his rope — and roar happily at his funny antics. Tex has been a big help as one of our Rodeo Judges.

"DUCKY" LaFountain — No matter where you look around the Ranch — there you'll find our "Ducky" — Cimarron's one-man F. B. I.!

"BOB" Tesnow — not only is he Jim Gunter's man "Friday" — but he plays a mean accordion besides!

"GUNNY" Wallgren — is the attractive reason your rooms are kept in apple-pie order — and what could be more important.

"BETTY" Curran — most of our fine help came originally to Cimarron as guests — Betty's father enjoyed the ranch - brought along his daughter - and here she is now "Round-Robining."

"FRITZ" and "ROBIN" Snyder — old time Cimarron Guests, are now next-door neighbors. Fritz is official RODEO TIMEKEEPER and Robin is editor-in-chief of this CIMARRON MAIL POUCH.

CIMARRON MAIL POUCH

THE WEEKS ARE FULL OF FUN AT CIMARRON

Monday — Riding Instructions in the Rodeo Arena. Ranch Movies in color and black & white, plus Western thrillers. Campfire Get-together.

Tuesday — Hay Ride — Up hill, down dale, under the country stars in an old-fashioned haytruck — with hay up to your ears!

Wednesday — Square Dance — in our Powder River Westerntown Hotel. If you've never enjoyed American folk dancing before — we'll teach you.

Thursday — Outdoor Picnic — by horseback to lovely Lake Oscawanna — swimming, canoeing, barbecue!

Friday — Each day of the week, our cowboys take you on an interesting trail ride — on Friday (and for Sunday services) you will visit Graymoor — the beautiful Franciscan Friars monastery, a world famous mecca for the faithful.

Saturday — Whoop-and-holler night in our Westerntown Last Chance Bar — Snack Grill — Powder River Hotel for Square Dancing and Fun!

Sunday — Church ride (optional). Afternoon Rodeo with guest participation games — Buffet Supper.

Before we seal the Mail Pouch — may we thank you sincerely for your patronage — may we wish you well — and may we remind you the big 4-day Thanksgiving Week-end marks the close of our 1950 Season. Hope we'll see you at the party — and again when we re-open in April 1951.

Sincerely,
CIMARRON

HARRY TOMPKINS
World's Champion Bull-rider

Have you ever been at Cimarron — to see the leaves turn gold?
When Autumn follows Summer — and its glories all unfold?
Have you ever been at Cimarron, when Summer heat begins to fade?
When over Putnam Valley, Beauty's hand is gently laid?
Have you ever been at Cimarron, when the air is crispy clear —
When during day, and into night, the touch of Fall is near?
When Nature dons new raiment, and living things change too —
When colors — bright and crystal clear, assume a softer hue.
It's then that Autumn follows Summer — Winter follows Fall —
Though — truly — ALL four Seasons, are a gift, from God, to all!

Adios — good friends!

GINNY BAIGAS
Cimarron Rodeo Queen

CIMARRON RANCH
PUTNAM VALLEY, N. Y.
TELEPHONE LAKELAND 8-8003
RETURN POSTAGE GUARANTEED

CIMARRON MAIL POUCH

CIMARRON RANCH   SPRING 1951   PUTNAM VALLEY, N. Y.

FIRST IN FUN FOR '51

We at Cimarron are attempting—by means of our Mail Pouch for Spring, 1951, to give you the FACTS about our Ranch. This Mail Pouch is intended as a simple, informative "GUIDE!" We sincerely hope the contents will be helpful—and will make enjoyable reading.

Cimarron will re-open for our THIRTEENTH season on FRIDAY, MARCH, 23rd, 1951, for Easter Week. Guest accommodations will then be available for weekends only during April and November. Full time, May thru October.

We are going to have an Easter Hat Parade, Saturday night, March 24th, with appropriate prizes for the three funniest homemade hats. One of the prizes is a free weekend . . . so . . . come join this fun parade.

We have been busy getting the ranch equipment . . . houses, barns, corral, Westerntown, etc., in "apple-pie" order. We are anxious that every detail of the ranch's operation will be in perfect condition when it is time to greet you, warmly, once again!

HOW DID CIMARRON ORIGINATE?

Cimarron Ranch was founded by Vern Walter, in 1939. Vern came East from his birthplace in the Badlands of South Dakota where he was raised on a ranch.

This thorough Western background and training fitted him to fulfill his ambition — to make his dream become a reality. He created — in the East — the FIRST REAL dude guest ranch.

It has taken thirteen years to make CIMARRON the FINEST Eastern-Western Wonderland—unequalled from coast to coast!

HOW IS CIMARRON OPERATED?

Cimarron is run by a staff which averages forty people—each one selected for his or her ability to perform their specific job. This group — most of whom have worked together year after year — consists of:

The Owner-Management — Office Staff — Barn Foreman and Wranglers — Entertainment Directors —Maintenance Men —Chef — Kitchen Help — Waitresses — Chambermaids —Rodeo and Riding Experts — Bartenders and Store Keepers —

All of whom have one desire — TO PLEASE YOU!

HOW IS CIMARRON REACHED?

Cimarron Ranch lies in Putnam Valley in the Taconic Mountain Range—the heart of Revolution country—still unspoiled and still incomparably beautiful. Springtime at Cimarron is especially lovely. The ranch acreage, and the whole surrounding countryside is a joy to ride over, walk through—live and relax in.

Driving from New York take parkways to Hawthorne Circle, thence toward Albany—pass the Peekskill exit—leave parkway at Shrub Oak—follow signs to Cimarron. From East take Route 6 to Shrub Oak—From New Jersey cross Bear Mt. Bridge toward Peekskill and follow signs to ranch —

For Out-of-New York Staters:

Take first through train or plane to New York City. (see the world's largest city enroute) Then take Sunday P. M. train from Grand Central Station in New York City, to PEEKSKILL where ranch car will meet train . . . Or . . . take through train from your starting point—get off at HARMON—where *all* trains stop to change engines. We will meet you there.

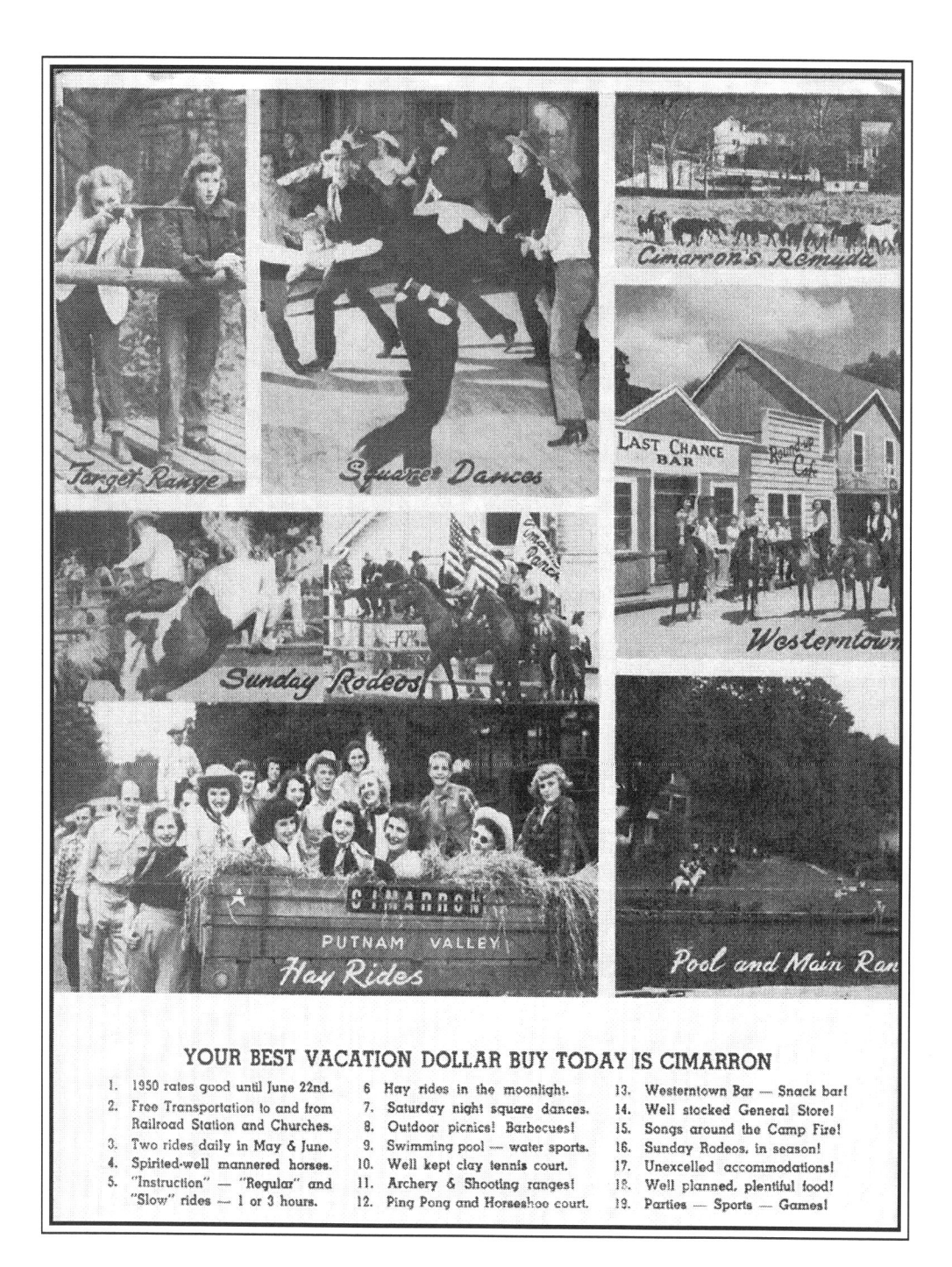

YOUR BEST VACATION DOLLAR BUY TODAY IS CIMARRON

1. 1950 rates good until June 22nd.
2. Free Transportation to and from Railroad Station and Churches.
3. Two rides daily in May & June.
4. Spirited-well mannered horses.
5. "Instruction" — "Regular" and "Slow" rides — 1 or 3 hours.
6. Hay rides in the moonlight.
7. Saturday night square dances.
8. Outdoor picnics! Barbecues!
9. Swimming pool — water sports.
10. Well kept clay tennis court.
11. Archery & Shooting ranges!
12. Ping Pong and Horseshoe court.
13. Westerntown Bar — Snack bar!
14. Well stocked General Store!
15. Songs around the Camp Fire!
16. Sunday Rodeos, in season!
17. Unexcelled accommodations!
18. Well planned, plentiful food!
19. Parties — Sports — Games!

- 178 -

PRE-SEASON RATES GOOD UNTIL JUNE 22nd.		Weekly	5 Weekdays	Weekends	Daily
MB—MEN'S BUNKHOUSE GD—GIRLS' DORMITORY		69.00 ea.	45.00 ea.	29.00 ea.	10.00 ea.
NB—PRIVATE ROOM with convenient baths	two in a room	77.00 ea.	50.00 ea.	32.00 ea.	11.00 ea.
CB—PRIVATE ROOM with connecting bath	two in a room	85.00 ea.	55.00 ea.	35.00 ea.	12.00 ea.
WB—PRIVATE ROOM with private bath	two in a room	89.00 ea.	57.00 ea.	37.00 ea.	13.00 ea.

Page Four

DIGEST OF THE "NEWS"

Ginny Bargas — our 1950 Eastern Dude Ranch Association Queen has been adding to the glamour (and helping with the chores) at Triple H Ranch, Tucson, Arizona.

Junie Buyhan — and his wife PAT are in Wyoming. They've been snowed in — have been hunting all winter — and are care-taking for T Cross Ranch.

Nena and Mark Barker — In Mesa, Arizona, Mark sought election to office. His initial political efforts did not succeed. Mark thanks all who voted for him — Nena thanks those who did not!

Kay and Dick Borden — are living with Kay's mother in Yonkers, N. Y., Kay lost her Dad — and we extend our condolences.

Ray Civerchia — wintered in his hometown of Peekskill. He'll be back at LAST CHANCE BAR to cheerfully and efficiently dispense refreshments.

Betty Curran — has also been in Tucson working at a ranch . . . and while there she married "Nooky" Eickler!

Frank Catandella — underwent a very serious operation. He is recuperating, perhaps the future holds happy plans for him and

Lee Wiims — who has been having operations on her foot — hurt last winter in an automobile accident. All is well now, and they will be married very soon.

Carol Fulton — is now Mrs. Earl Casey, living near her Army husband in the South.

Ollie Flanner — as usual, took care of Cimarron all winter. She'll be back

CIMARRON MAIL POUCH

again behind our Westerntown Snack Bar.

Bill Gullick — has been basking in the West Palm Beach sun, building energy to resume charge of Cimarron's kitchen.

Gunay Wallgren — and her "Bob" have marriage plans — still another ranch romance.

Chris Zebroski — can't decide whether she is a Tucsonite or a New Yorker since Tucson has been her winterhaven for so long now.

Frank & Betty Garsamom — have been shoveling their way through the snow out of their lovely home in Putnam Valley.

Bobbie Gitkin — hangs his riding hat in Oregon Corners — to be near Cimarron.

Jim Gunter — kept the home fires brightly burning until Lu and Vern returned from Florida. Then he went traveling around to visit his many friends.

Lu and Vern Walter — after one of Cimarron's busiest seasons enjoyed a well-earned vacation in Florida and are back at the ranch ready and anxious to extend hospitality to old and new friends.

Sue Waitelis — Cancelled her winter plans and cared for her ill mother and in February married one of our handsome guests "Brad" Rogers. 15 other Cimarron employees were involved in romances last season.

Marjorie Giblin — paid us a November visit from Burbank, California, which she now calls "home."

Marie Hill — has been a busy and happy career girl in Washington D.C.

Bart Hilber — is making good in radio and television. At the Fall Rodeo Party his talents were proven.

Terry Haussman — was on our staff end of last season. Has left for Old Bridge, New Jersey.

Mike Hastings — wintered — as always — at Cimarron. He won't turn over the care of our horses to anyone else — so our "string" is in fine form and 'racin' to go.

Al Kaur — has been in Brooklyn, and we understand has a fine job.

Bob Kamps — is still in Tokyo, Japan. His Mary and the five boys may have to be evacuated to the States.

Elsie Lehmann — has been living in New York City — designing textiles and such —

Gene McBride — stayed at Cimarron during the winter — assisting Mike Hastings.

Sylvia Noel — stayed with her sister in Albany, New York. She will be in charge of the Silver Saddle Trading Post again!

Zip Peterson — married Ginnie Worden in December — another ranch romance. Honeymooning in Arizona.

Hank Ritcono — has been sliding on ice and snow in Putnam Valley, to drop in at the ranch occasionally.

Dad Walter — accompanied Lu and Vern to Miami; enjoying the Florida sunshine and warmth —

Alyce & Stanley Walter — joined the rest of the gang at Tucson, and will be back with us for the 1951 season — —

Bob Tesnow — left in the Fall to join his "Gunny" in Florida —

Robin Snyder — editor of Cimarron Mail Pouch — wintered in sunny Naples, Florida.

CIMARRON RANCH
PUTNAM VALLEY, N. Y.
Telephone LAkeland 8-8003

Return Postage Guaranteed

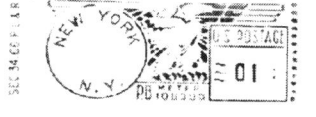

- 180 -

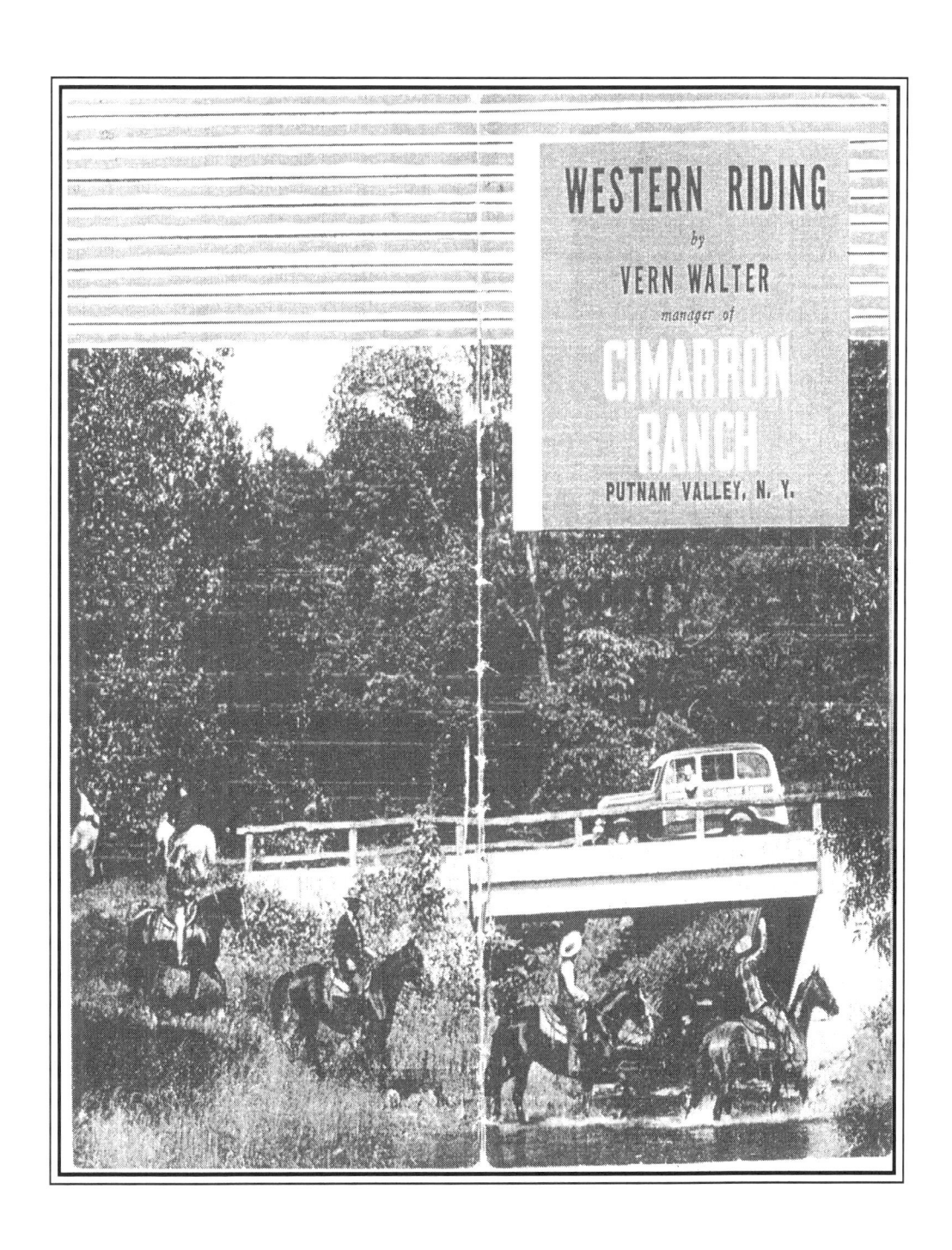

Riding Book written by Vern Walter at Cimarron Ranch

may be some fault of your own which we can help you to correct.

You will find horseback riding really exhilarating, but there are things to learn and skills to acquire, just as there are in any other active sport, so, for your safety and utmost enjoyment (and there is plenty), you must exercise caution in selecting your riding group, mounting and dismounting your horse and remain constantly alert while you are in the saddle.

All rides are in groups of approximately ten riders, in charge of a capable wrangler. You may ride by yourself, if Mike Hastings, the corral boss, considers you an experienced rider, if you know the trails, and you want to pay extra for the private use of a horse.

The rides leave at 9:30 A. M., and 2:30 P. M., to a different point of interest each day. It would take a month of daily riding to cover all the different scenic trails that radiate in all directions from the ranch. We try to have the rides back an hour before meals, in time for a shower, a swim, or a cocktail at the LAST CHANCE SALOON. When you return to the ranch after the ride, see that your horse gets a drink, then take him away from the trough, dismount, wrap the reins around the saddle horn and he will go to his stall.

Generous applications of a pest control insecticide are continually "fogged" around the ranch and along many of the trails, but if flies bother your horse, get a branch and brush them off your mount's head.

Do not allow your horse to "ride up" on the horse ahead. He may step on the other's heels, which is mighty painful and may cause him to kick in self-defense . . . and he may hit you on the shins which is also mighty painful.

Relax in the saddle as soon as you can. Alternately touching the horse's head and then his tail with your free hand as you start off at a walk will help you to relax.

Do not ride with excessive weight on one stirrup. It pulls the saddle against the horse's withers causing saddle sores. If you swing around to look backwards, let most of your weight fall in the center of the saddle.

The natural gaits of a saddle horse are . . . walk, trot, and gallop. A slow gallop (collected canter) is called a "lope." It is the most enjoyable gait to ride and not too hard on your horse, and we lope along whenever the going is suitable.

Riding abreast is the normal cowboy style. But, for your safety's sake, and to take advantage of the softest part of the trail, we insist on galloping *single file only* . . . and no passing is permitted while galloping.

Two thirds of all horseback accidents on or off ranches occur in mounting and dismounting by inexperienced riders. When horses are saddled in the morning, the saddle girth is not tightened sufficiently for riding. Shortly before a rider is ready to mount, the wrangler tightens the girth. Do not mount until you are sure the girth has been tightened. Have the wranglers teach you how tight your girth should be for safe riding, and always test it yourself before mounting. Unless you are an experienced horseman, do not attempt to tighten the girth yourself before you mount or loosen it when you dismount. There is definitely a correct way to mount a horse, besides just climbing into the saddle. Have the wrangler show you how to mount and dismount. Never, in dismounting from a Western saddle, kick your feet free and slide down the side of the saddle and your horse.

Do not make sudden and unexpected motions around a horse's head. He may, instinctively, jump back or sideways.

If you should fall off, don't blame the poor beast. He can't argue back and chances are you were partially at fault.

If you've always ridden "English," that's fine and it's a wonderful way to ride in the proper environment. But that is usually not the case on a ranch where you may be riding fairly steep hills, or into the high country where you are really climbing. It takes an expert English rider to ride steep trails without letting his weight slip too far back in the saddle where it rests over the horse's kidneys, which can result in injury to the horse.

On many of our ranch rides, it is advisable to carry a light coat or sweater. It can be tied on the saddle, if you don't want to wear it. There is, of course, no place on an English saddle to tie on a wrap, or a slicker in case of rain. So . . . if you will take our advice, you will be content to ride as the rest of us do . . . in a Western saddle. And, if you will let us help you on the first ride or two, you will find yourself riding just as comfortable, if not far more so, than in any other type of saddle.

Your "seat" in a Western saddle is almost exactly opposite that used for English riding. An English saddle has so little leather between you and the horse, that you ride easily with a thigh grip, and, of course, that is your security on such a saddle. The Western saddle has so many thicknesses of leather between you and the horse, that it is uncomfortable to ride with any sort of a "leg grip." A rider can post on a Western saddle, but, instead of trying to leg grip, we ride more by balance, using a longer stirrup, with the ball of the foot in the stirrup, the heels down, and "sitting" the saddle on a trot instead of posting. Or, you may stand in the stirrups and bend slightly forward but with your knees free of any pressure on the horse. It is not a difficult technique to learn and we would be glad to give you all the instructions you wish. Most riders master this very quickly.

English riding apparel is usually not too comfortable, but most of us, for ranch riding, wear denims and cowboy boots. However, you can ride a Western saddle in slacks or anything that's comfortable; and even good substantial shoes, jodphur boots or ordinary oxfords can be worn without discomfort. If you are wearing jeans or slacks, I strongly recommend that you also wear a pair of old-time old-style long "undies" from the waist to the ankle, at least for the first few rides. Otherwise, you may get the inside of your knees scuffed up a bit. The undies should be of medium weight but always ankle length, never knee length. If you have bruised legs, you can get the proper medication at the ranch.

Sit in your saddle erect and alert; *keep your heels down* an inch or two lower than the ball of your foot. Pull in the small of your back, get your chest out and hold your head erect, and pull in your stomach. You can do it — and still be relaxed. Horseback riding is rated next to swimming in the beneficial use and exercise of the largest number of muscles in the body — but to get the benefit of this, you must sit your horse properly, erect and alert, but without tension.

If you are wearing a large hat or a loose scarf, be careful to see that they are securely fastened so as not to fly off in the face of an incoming horse which may shy and throw his rider.

Don't permit your horse to go to sleep under you — which is entirely possible. Maintain a light contact on the reins with your horse's mouth ... not pulling, but keeping him awake and alert. Use your heels, if necessary, if your horse seems to get sluggish.

Don't allow your mount to lag behind the riders in front. Horses are gregarious; they like to be fairly close to one another. If, through carelessness, they are allowed to drop far behind, they may suddenly break into a gallop to catch up with the horses in front. Always be in thoughtful control of your horse.

If your horse stumbles and goes to his knees, don't get panicky. Nine times out of ten, he will regain his feet. Pick him up with your reins but don't jerk his head up. Help him with a firm but gentle pull on the reins and the minute you see he is regaining his feet, stop pulling him, slack off on the reins, and just maintain contact with his mouth. If you continue to pull back on your reins after he is on his feet, he may back into other horses or rear up in an attempt to relieve himself of the painful pressure on his mouth.

Most of our horseback fun is riding beautiful trails running in all directions from the ranch. The wrangler who leads your group is in charge of the ride. His place is at the head of the column and the pace he sets should be observed by all the riders in the party.

The wrangler will do his best to keep an eye on everyone but much will depend on the "trail courtesy" of each rider. Keep at least 3 or 4 feet back of the horse ahead of you. Do not hold back, and if you desire to return to the ranch, get permission from the wrangler before leaving the group.

Keep your eyes open for unusual objects lying beside the trail. They may frighten your horse or a sudden gust of wind may shift them towards your horse causing him to jump sideways and unseat you. If you use half the alertness in riding a horse that you use in driving an automobile on the highway, you will probably be safer on your horse than you are in your car.

Do not let your horse eat while riding on the trail, and never start your mount into a fast trot or gallop without warning the riders ahead first. There may be inexperienced riders whose horses will break into an unexpected gallop when they hear your horse coming up. Also, it is courtesy to wait for a rider who has dismounted to open or shut a gate or pick up any article from the ground.

Don't tie your horse to a hitching rail by the reins. Wrap them loosely around a rail ... or pair off the horses and tie the reins to each others left stirrup, quite short, so that they won't get "fouled up."

Keep clear of the heels of all horses. A perfectly quiet, gentle, well-mannered horse, may be suddenly frightened at the head . . . or should a bee sting him . . . or any unexpected event occur . . . the horse, gentle as he may be, may suddenly kick or fly backwards.

Only curb bits are used on ranch horses. This requires riding with a slightly loose rein, which should be tightened gradually when stopping or slowing down. Jerking the reins causes horses acute pain and ruins their mouths.

Always walk your horse for five minutes when starting on a ride, making sure that your "gear" is right and get the feel of your mount. Also for at least five minutes at the end of a ride, to "cool him out" so he can drink and eat.

Never run your horse up or down hills. Watch your horse as you go down short, sharp inclines. Every horse is inclined to trot down such inclines. If you permit your horse to do this, he may stumble over a rolling stone and fall. Hold your pony in check, make him walk down grades. Always keep your horse at a walk over rough, stony ground. A rocky trail or hard road is hard on a horse's feet and legs.

Do not gallop for more than four or five minutes at a stretch; it takes only one or two hard, fast runs to tire your horse when you are on a long ride.

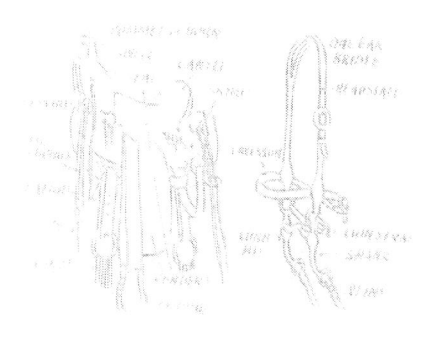

Only in Western novels do people gallop "endlessly over the prairies." A cowpuncher on a round-up has a string of horses like a polo player.

Sunday afternoon is Rodeo Day at Cimarron. If you wish to compete for prizes in the guests' games, you must sign a Rodeo Liability Release at the office before noon on Sunday.

We are glad to have the children ride; glad to instruct them and safeguard them in every possible way. When there is a sufficient group of children, we prefer to have wranglers take them out by themselves.

During dry times, we are in a highly hazardous fire area. A carelessly thrown match or cigarette can start a fire instantly, particularly in the Fall months. At times, smoking is not allowed on the trails. Your wrangler will stop at designated places on the ride where smoking is permitted. Your cooperation is greatly appreciated.

These suggestions and the few other regulations in effect at the ranch are solely for the safety and pleasure of all our guests.

Vern Walter.

WE ARE ONE OF THE CHARTER MEMBERS OF THE EASTERN DUDE RANCHERS ASSOCIATION.

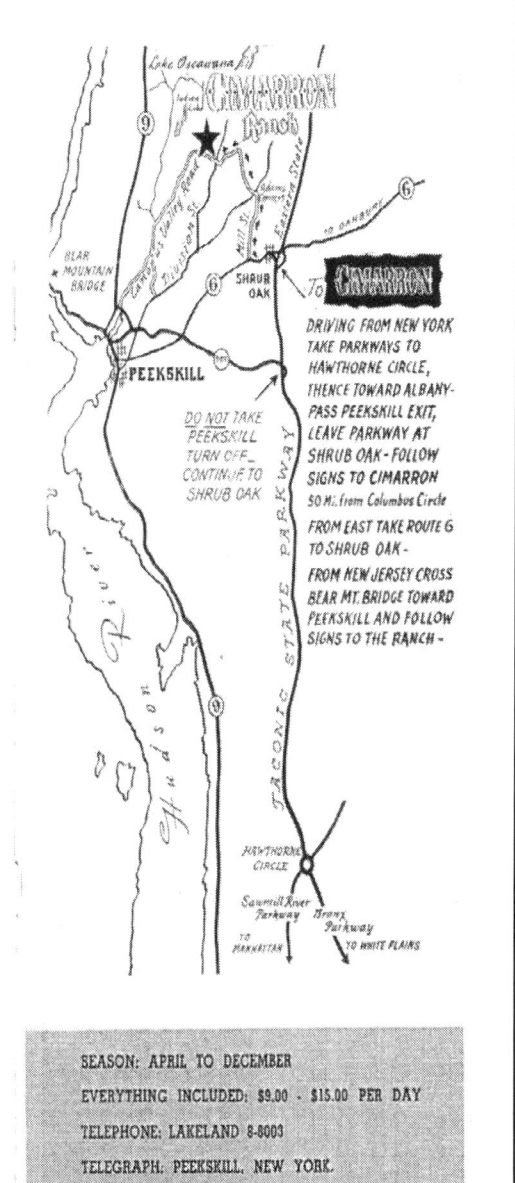

DRIVING FROM NEW YORK TAKE PARKWAYS TO HAWTHORNE CIRCLE, THENCE TOWARD ALBANY-PASS PEEKSKILL EXIT, LEAVE PARKWAY AT SHRUB OAK - FOLLOW SIGNS TO CIMARRON
50 Mi. from Columbus Circle

FROM EAST TAKE ROUTE 6 TO SHRUB OAK -

FROM NEW JERSEY CROSS BEAR MT. BRIDGE TOWARD PEEKSKILL AND FOLLOW SIGNS TO THE RANCH -

SEASON: APRIL TO DECEMBER
EVERYTHING INCLUDED: $9.00 - $15.00 PER DAY
TELEPHONE: LAKELAND 8-8003
TELEGRAPH: PEEKSKILL, NEW YORK.
ADDRESS: PUTNAM VALLEY, NEW YORK.

CIMARRON MAIL POUCH

CIMARRON RANCH   SPRING 1947   PEEKSKILL, N.Y.

JOIN THE FUN AT CIMARRON

Happier Holidays for You

About 50 years ago, Western ranchers were visited by their Eastern relatives and friends, who were completely fascinated by the carefree, outdoor life of the open range, so much so, that they insisted upon returning year after year as paying guests—and thus was born the present dude ranch industry.

"Dude Ranchers" was the name given to the Western ranchers when they accommodated their Eastern cousins, who were humorously termed "dudes," and little entertainment was provided for the guests except horseback riding.

Raised in the land of the pioneer dude ranches, Vern Walter brought the idea East and started the first Eastern Dude Ranch in New York State in the early nineteen thirties—creating a business that was immediately accepted and which, today, ranks high in the choice of vacationists.

In elaborating on dude ranching, the Eastern ranches provided other entertainment as well as riding. However, realizing that the biggest expense of dude ranching lies in horses, their care, equipment and upkeep, it has been the tendency of many ranchers to sharply limit the amount of riding time provided to the guests. Therefore, when choosing a dude ranch, it would be well to determine the amount of riding guaranteed under their rates. At Cimarron we give each guest a 3 hour riding period, plus entertainment—still maintaining, however, enough horses to provide extra riding, or the exclusive use of a horse at a slight additional charge.

A LIFE OF THRILLING ROMANCE AND CHARM AWAITS YOU

It is the sincere desire of everyone connected with Cimarron to see that your 1947 visit at the ranch stands out as a never-to-be-forgotten event in your life.

Your accommodation, whether bunkhouse or room with private bath, will be the last word in comfort, and clean as a whistle, too.

The food will be the best that money can buy, expertly prepared and carefully served to you in our new, large, gayly-decorated dining room.

Westerntown will continue to be our "Whoop and Holler" rendezvous. There will be something doing all the time and an expertly-called square dance twice a week.

You will find the horses fat and sassy, well-fed and cared for by that expert horseman and all-around cowboy, Mike Hastings.

NO EXPENSE HAS BEEN SPARED

We firmly believe we have the finest string of dude ranch horses to be found anywhere. Last year we bought over two carloads of excellent stock, bringing our total to over a hundred saddle horses. We have carefully culled the "bad actors" and "hard riders" out of the string, until now we have a remuda of which we are justifiably proud.

Resting—Relaxing and Refreshing

Enjoy this Carefree Dude Ranch Life

Fondest Childhood Dreams Come True

Join Us and Let the Cares of the World Go By

You are met at the Peekskill station by the ranch driver, and driven the eight miles to the ranch over the beautiful rolling hillsides of Putnam Valley. At the foot of a steep hill, you enter the ranch buildings, and your driver lets you out at the office door. After registering at the desk, you are shown to your accommodations and given the opportunity to become acquainted with the general layout of the ranch; namely, the location of the dining-room, playroom, Westerntown, Rodeo Arena and ranch stables.

Let's assume you arrive on Sunday P. M.—you will be put on the Monday morning ride, and after breakfast, (you will be assigned to a table for your stay) you will follow the crowd, through Westerntown, around the Rodeo arena, to the barns, where Mike will pick out a horse for you.

If you have requested the instruction ride, you will be taken into the rodeo arena where the fundamentals of horseback riding are explained and demonstrated to you. Each guest is taught how to control his horse and the position to assume which will insure the most comfort and safety during all the horse's gaits. When you have mastered control of your horse, you will be taken out on the trails, for further instruction.

You may choose the intermediate ride which is recommended for those who haven't ridden recently, or for beginners in Western-style riding. This ride goes out on the trails at once, trotting and galloping for short distances, with helpful hints from your cowboy instructor.

The regular ride is for those experienced in ranch-style riding, and usually goes to some popular point of interest.

Whichever ride you choose, you will return to the ranch in ample time to "freshen up" for lunch.

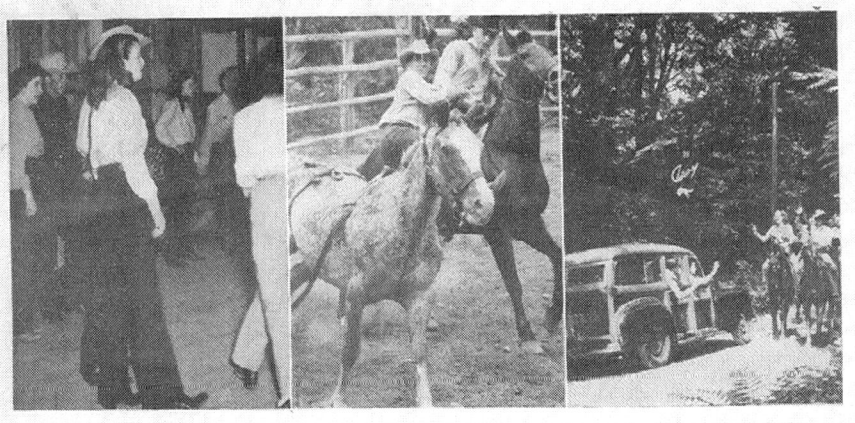

Pick Your Partner and Promenade   *See A Wild West Rodeo*   *Adios Amigo — Hasta LaVista*

Cimarron Ranch – The Eastern Western Wonderland

After lunch, while you relax in the coolness of the shade trees on the front lawn, you can select your afternoon activity—group entertainment is scheduled, but you may prefer to sun bathe by the pool, take a swim, play tennis, shoot archery, pitch quoits, try target practise, climb a mountain, join the fun in Westerntown, write some letters, play ping pong or just rest, for there is a big evening's entertainment ahead—a sort of a "get acquainted" party!

Tuesday you will most likely be scheduled for the afternoon ride, so sleep late if you like, and breakfast, at your pleasure, at the Round-up Cafe in Westerntown.

In the afternoon, choose the type ride that suits you best. Remember, it's square-dance night in Powder River Hotel, and inasmuch as we call this a "warm-up dance" for the big Saturday night event, your caller will carefully explain the "allemande left" and other common square dance calls to assist you in mastering this popular dance of the range.

The next day, you will be at the barn early to be on with your horseback riding, and, after an afternoon of fun, and a Supper of special delight, you'll be anxious to get to the rodeo arena as this is the night for the dress rehearsal of the big Sunday Rodeo. Ranch hands will practise their mounted quadrille—yes, a square dance done on horseback—and the boys will "buck-out" some of the rodeo stock for your entertainment. After the rodeo, there may be a hay ride planned that you won't want to miss.

Thursday is picnic day. Half go by horseback, and the balance by truck, to enjoy a meal cooked in the open, and a swim in the crystal-clear water of a mountain lake. If you went over on the truck, you would return by horseback and, after supper, you will enjoy an evening's entertainment of movies, a Western thriller, or maybe colored movies of the ranch.

Friday, you may choose the ride that is going to a spot of special interest to you—the Monastery at Graymoor, the "Bird and Bottle Inn" at Garrison, or a ride to Moonlight Ridge. There will be a campfire at the ranch that night, and songs of welcome for the new arrivals.

The ranch assumes a carnival air on Saturday. Rodeo hands arrive for the Sunday show, and it's a regular Western Saturday night. Cowboys and cowgirls all "duded up" for the big "hoe down." The orchestra tunes up and the caller sings out "Get your hair in a braid and let's get going!"

On Sunday morning, there is a horseback ride to Mass, or you may go in the ranch car. When you return, you will see the rodeo arena all decked out in flags which means "Rodeo this Afternoon." So—after a sumptuous Sunday dinner, you go to the arena, where seats have been reserved for you, and while Sunday afternoon is "horse holiday" at the ranch, our rodeo stock gets more than its share of work to do. Here you may cheer on your favorite cowboy or cowgirl as they compete for prize money in the various events. The show starts with a colorful Grand Entry of officials, contestants, and guest participants, followed by the "riding of the colors" and introduction of officials. Then comes that thrilling "dance of the range," the horseback quadrille, ridden by six couples, of ranch hands. Contest and special events follow to the Grand Finale, the rough and tumble wild steer race. The show lasts about two hours and is packed with laughs, thrills and spills from the beginning to the end. It's a real Western show! Typical, indeed, of the life and atmosphere of Cimarron!

If time permits, and you can be with us longer, you will find each succeeding week more interesting and fun-packed than the last, but if you must go home Sunday night, we will arrange for your transportation to the station, and bid you a fond farewell, with the sincere hope that we will meet again and again.

Cimarron takes your vacation seriously. We feel it a deep responsibility, for perhaps you have waited a year for this outing. We, therefore, strive to the utmost to make it a memorable one!

Page 4   CIMARRON RANCH

Cimarron Brings You All The Glitter And Glamour Of Grand Living   *A Vacation Of Treasured*

Cimarron is managed with expert skill, based on long years of experience. Now enjoying our ninth season, we are justly proud of our good name. Folks tell us they can't explain just what it is, but there is an air of "know how" about the way all things are taken care of.

"Dude Ranching" does appeal to people of all ages, but being an active outdoor life, it, naturally, attracts a greater percentage of young folks. But, regardless of your age, you are sure to find companions and a wide variety of sports and entertainment to suit you perfectly.

All the riding is under constant supervision from the moment Mike selects a horse for you, a cowboy assists you to mount and whethe. choose the regular ride, the inte   de or the instruction ride. A
teresting trails are

Cupids Bow For A Gal In Calico    *Double The Thrill—On Two*    *Moon Is Low, Campfires Glow*

Author's note: Last Brochure from Cimarron Ranch - It must be a printers proof or first run - and we can't read some of the lines.

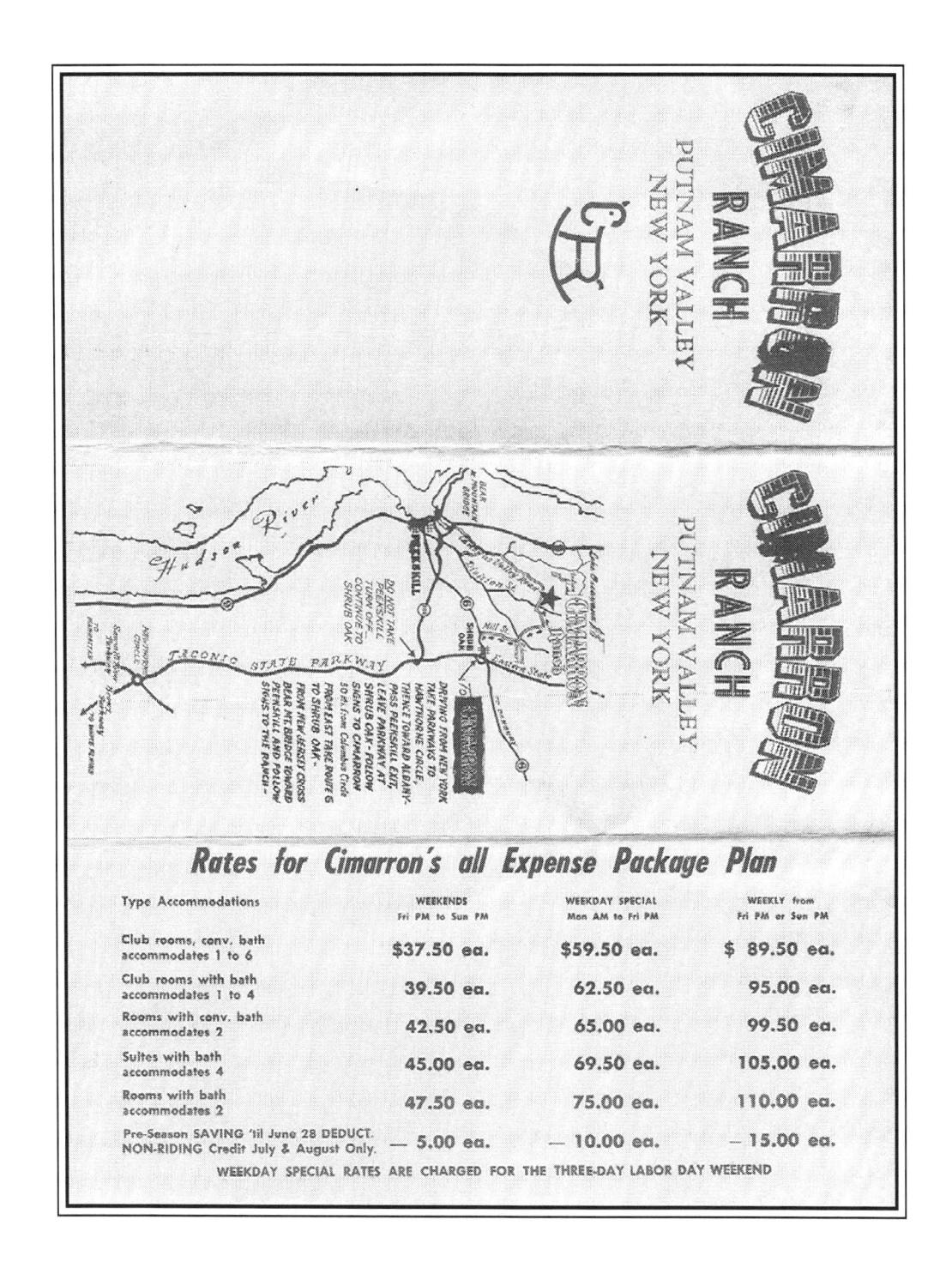

CIMARRON RANCH
PUTNAM VALLEY, NEW YORK

Rates for Cimarron's all Expense Package Plan

Type Accommodations	WEEKENDS Fri PM to Sun PM	WEEKDAY SPECIAL Mon AM to Fri PM	WEEKLY from Fri PM or Sun PM
Club rooms, conv. bath accommodates 1 to 6	$37.50 ea.	$59.50 ea.	$89.50 ea.
Club rooms with bath accommodates 1 to 4	39.50 ea.	62.50 ea.	95.00 ea.
Rooms with conv. bath accommodates 2	42.50 ea.	65.00 ea.	99.50 ea.
Suites with bath accommodates 4	45.00 ea.	69.50 ea.	105.00 ea.
Rooms with bath accommodates 2	47.50 ea.	75.00 ea.	110.00 ea.
Pre-Season SAVING 'til June 28 DEDUCT. NON-RIDING Credit July & August Only.	— 5.00 ea.	— 10.00 ea.	— 15.00 ea.

WEEKDAY SPECIAL RATES ARE CHARGED FOR THE THREE-DAY LABOR DAY WEEKEND

1963 IS CIMARRON'S 25th ANNIVERSARY

Lu and Vern Walter, with Betty and Frank Garramone, ranch owners, are celebrating this year for ~~YOU who have made this happy event possible. We've learned your likes and dislikes, so, with our Grand Opening on Saturday, May 18th, and continuing through the summer, we dedicate ourselves to empha~~size the things that make your ranch vacation a most memorable and happy event.

> CIMARRON is lively and it will be livelier.
>
> ~~CIMARRON is hospitable and will be more so.~~
>
> ~~CIMARRON is clean and will be kept so.~~
>
> CIMARRON'S food is good, and will be tastier.
>
> CIMARRON'S horses are perfect, you will agree.
>
> CIMARRON'S sports' activities will be improved.
>
> CIMARRON'S entertainment program will be better.
>
> CIMARRON'S rates are fair and will continue so.
>
> CIMARRON'S location is perfect, so we won't move.

Why don't you dial our direct-to-the-ranch, New York City telephone number, LOrraine 2-7777, or Putnam Valley, LAkeland 8-8003, and reserve accommodations for a weekend (Friday PM to Sunday PM) . . . our Economy Weekday Special (Monday AM to Friday PM) . . . for a week or more, or just come any day for a "Cimarron Sampler," from after breakfast to after supper, 2 meals, horseback riding, with all sports and entertainment, for only $10.00 on weekdays, $12.50 for Saturdays, Sundays and Holidays, until July 1st ($12.50 - $15.00 in season).

THIS IS CELEBRATION YEAR at CIMARRON

Learn to Ride Horseback...

Horseback riding instructions are free to all ranch guests. Printed "Tips on Riding" plus "Dos and Don'ts for Dudes" are availabe and a helpful starter. Next, a few minutes on our mechanical horse helps you to get the feeling of a horse in motion. Your instructor then takes you in the ranch arena on horseback, properly adjusts your stirrups and riding position, and demonstrates the simple signals which control your mount, giving you confidence and enabling you to relax and enjoy the wonderful sport of horseback riding. Beginners are conducted on short trail rides :.. first at a walk ... then on a trot ... and finally on a comfortable gallup, the next gait of a horse. When you "get your seat" at a lope, you move up to the intermediate riding group, and, in a week's time, many new riders are found on the regular ride.

Horseback riding is a pleasant way to participate in our President's Physical Fitness Endeavor ... beats walkin' 50 miles! When you consider the hours of enjoyment on horseback, the traveling time and expense you save, and the relaxed and informal ranch living, there is no vacation-resort as rewarding as a few days at Cimarron Ranch, in Putnam Valley, New York. Many people are regular weekend guests ... after ten weekends "the next one is on us."

GET THE CIMARRON HABIT... YOU'LL BE GLAD YOU DID!

BIRDSEYE OF CIMARRON RANCH - BY GOLLY — By Ollie

CIMARRON'S ALL EXPENSE PACKAGE PLAN INCLUDES

parking space for your car, or transportation from and to the Peekskill Railroad Station (8 miles—the taxi fare is $3.50) . . . your accommodations, horseback riding, 3 meals daily, all sports and entertainment, group riding instructions, plus transportation to Sunday Church Services.

Space is limited Therefore, a ten-dollar deposit, per person, guarantees accommodations. Deposit will be refunded on one week's cancellation notice.

When requesting reservations, please state 2nd choice, if possible.

ROOMS AVAILABLE AFTER SUPPER. RESERVATION DEPOSIT WILL BE CONFIRMED.

A Cimarron Ranch Vacation

Cimarron Ranch nestles, snugly, in the hills of the Taconic Mountain Range... only 50 miles north of New York City ... a yet unspoiled urban area where remaining early country markers of the Revolution and the New York to Albany stage coach route readily transform you thousands of miles from the bustling city. Clear, fresh country air rising over the mountain ridges is why the location is referred to as the "normally cooler northern area"... Modern parkways afford easy access to all areas. Train travel is also convenient. The ranch wagon meets you at Peekskill station, which is on the main line of the New York Central. (on prior notification) ... You will receive a friendly welcome at the ranch...assignment to your proper riding group... scheduled for a horseback ride to mass at Graymoor if you desire... and conducted to your accommodations by a cheerful ranch employee. Hastily, you'll get out of your city attire, don Levis or sports clothes, which are "formal" for your vacation at Cimarron. A trip to "Westerntown" (The fun center of the ranch) immediately puts you in the swing of ranch gaiety... dancing and entertainment conducted by the ranch social director...

**This was the inside of the brochure - It was large newspaper size.
It has been reduced to fit in the book.**

Hee-Haw at Gas Rationing

By DON SHORT.

PEEKSKILL, N. Y., May 13.—Until some bright young economist can think up a reason for rationing oats, life in the rustic rendezvous of Westerntown here at Cimarron Ranch will go on as usual. Every horse I interviewed here today expressed not only a lack of interest in gasoline, but a positive disdain for the stuff.

Unless my horse-language interpreter was doing a bit of romancing, those hearty whinnies which echoed from the long barn back of the big corral held a note of cynicism. I am quite certain that the fiery steed which carried me over and around these Putnam Hills the other day stuck out his chest just a wee bit and stepped a little more pridefully over the rocks and through the rivers.

A careful interpreter of equine thoughts would have had no trouble reading such mental mumblings as:

"So you thought I was through, eh? All washed up. A has-been. Well, why don't you laugh any more when they pull that old wheeze about 'Get a horse'?"

I have heard some horse laughs in my time and I assure you these bragging bronchos are positively guffawing.

All of this has served only to increase the delights of dude ranching here in Putnam Valley, just an hour from New York, or 99 cents worth of New York Central service. The steaks are juicy, the air bracing and the informality disarming. The Saturday evening square dances have lost none of their flavor or fervor, with gay caballeros and chic cabalulus bowing, hopping and swingin' their pardners to the rythym of a three-piece mountain symphony.

* * *

Two years ago, almost to the day, I had my introduction to this 3,000 acre slice of the old West, brought East by Vern Walter. Cimarron has grown bigger and it now has a little brother, Cinnabar, but the completely Western flavor of the spot has never changed.

Westerntown, the unique rangeland village, has weathered and aged just enough to make the illusion complete. Summer evenings find the dances under way at the Powder River Hotel with the Last Chance Saloon, the Roundup Cafe and the Silver Saddle Trading Post doing a rushing business. The wooden sidewalk echoes to the heels of high cowboy boots and the nodding horses at the hitching rail complete a scene that might have been lifted bodily from any Hollywood horse opera.

Daytime, when the bright sunlight brings out the full beauty of the valley, the bands of horsemen and horsewomen trotting down the dusty street in chaps, "Levis" and sombreros, the cowboys herding stray mounts in through the corral gate and the old stage coach rumbling out over the wooden bridge bound for Cinnabar, all combine to hold realities of the surrounding world in the background and convince the beholder that time has truly pulled the curtain on years past.

The last time I came up here, my horse-companion was a towering grayish animal, aptly named "Ironsides." This time I won "Roundup" in the corral raffle. He proved a much more cooperative mount, with the result that some three hours after we rode out of Cimarron, "Roundup" and I returned, having achieved complete harmony of purpose.

There are easy rides for beginners, instructions for all who seek them, long mountain trails to test the skill of more experienced riders; tennis courts for those who want to distribute their charley-horses evenly; a swimming pool; a lake; and the great indoors for when it rains.

The pink and white blossoms of the dogwood, the lavender of the lilacs have sprinkled Putnam Valley with color to highlight the pale green of the new foliage.

Cimarron is a picture at this season—a pretty picture, sans transportation headaches.

Travel

Centerfold Ad from 1953 Madison Square Garden Rodeo Brochure

RRON RANCH

PUTNAM VALLEY 1, NEW YORK

SPACIOUS DINING ROOM

REAL WESTERN TOWN

IT'S WESTERN!

DAILY — WEEKLY — WEEKEND ACCOMMODATIONS AVAILABLE

RESERVATIONS SUGGESTED — TELEPHONE LAKELAND 8-8003

VSR *finest whiskey of all the blends!*

THREE FEATHERS — Very Special Reserve

BLENDED WHISKEY · 86.8 PROOF · 65% GRAIN NEUTRAL SPIRITS
THREE FEATHERS DISTILLING COMPANY, ALADDIN, PA.

SPRINGTIME AT CIMARRON
Ready - and Waiting - for YOU!

Cimarron Ranch Newsletter - Retyped pages:

At the time of this writing, most of us are completely "fed up" with the rigors of Winter. Nothing has gone exactly right for too many discouraging days. We are all pretty sick of the seemingly everlasting cold, snow, sleet and ice typical of months of an unusually long season, resulting in all the big, and little irritations that mount daily. You and I are thoroughly tired of our overshoes, our intermittent "colds" and the increasingly difficult effort of maintaining a false enthusiasm for the simple task of living from day to day. Our usual "Pep" has disappeared. All that we have left is the protective urge to "get away from it all" but quickly.

We look out our windows and see nothing but soot-blackened snow, gutters of muddy water, trees - once lovely, presenting now bare forlorn branches, stretching leafless arms in apparent hopeless yearning; gray, uncertain skies above; a panorama discouraged and in state of undecided pause.

To reverse all this gloom and to quote a very apt phrase "IF WINTER COMES - CAN SPRING BE FAR BEHIND?" The answer is a most hopeful and emphatic "No - it can't"! The waiting tonic to our jaded spirits lives very, very close at hand.

Within swift and convenient train distance from New York City lies Cimarron Ranch, in lovely Putnam Valley. And there awaits you, the first, fresh, bright days of spring. Just picture yourself walking through Cimarron's corral on your way to the big white barn, all set for your morning ride. The sun will give promise of consoling warmth. The stirring breezes will ensure cool, refreshing winds. You'll walk into the barn and it will be all so familiar and friendly once again. The horses will be saddled and waiting and they will remember you, never fear - that's one of the nice things about horses. They'll be as anxious as you to re-discover the trails you both know, to feel and see again another springtime miracle of a world vividly emerging, with a fresh and inspiring courage from the confining embrace of winter.

Then, you, the friends you'll meet again, and the horse of your choice will find yourselves on Continental Village Road. Just ahead, on your right when you've passed Cimarron's lovely waterfall, nestles quaint, old "Sundown." Did you ever stop to think about "Sundown?" It's a white, authentic Colonial - true - but it's more than one of the Ranch's guesthouses in which you may have spent many happy times. It's as much a part of the historic countryside as the land on which it has stood for some one hundred and fifty-odd years - ever since the American Revolutionary days. That was when the British overran and burned the Valley in which you ride. The house itself was deeded to the original owners, the Hortons. The ridges surrounding it, up toward which you look and whose slopes you ride, are the sites of old iron mines, essential in those Revolutionary War days to the manufacturers of cannon and ball for our Continental armies. Perhaps on this lovely Spring morning, you'll turn off to your left directly in front of "Sundown's" white slat fence, through the wooden gate into the pasture. That pasture, where the ride has stopped so many times to adjust stirrups and divide the rider by their own choice into fast and slow groups, is more than a grazing field and fenced corral for Cimarron's horses. It's also the site of the resting place, just ahead of you a bit, of the Hortons. You may never have noticed that just before you lope through the first stone boundary, there are tall trees set in a square, enclosing the family burial ground of the Hortons. Walk into it, one spring morning, if only to sense the imperturbable serenity of the little plot. The crumbled stones of past generations are still there, a few of them legible, but you won't feel sad- its all too finally restful and at peace.

Then, along the brook's banks, bubbling again after their confinement, you'll see the first, definite signs of spring and the summer to follow. Not the red winged blackbirds, the blue jays, nor the starlings winging their glad way above you, but down close along the banks and the road as well, the startling green of the skunk cabbage. It's a pretty and a brave plant, with it's cowl-shaped leaves, deserving of a more romantic name. After all, it is so-called because it emerges hopeful and alert during the mating season of the little weasel with the same name.

Astride your horse as you lope along, look about you at the old, gnarled apple trees straining to burst forth into exquisite blossoms and later into fruit, purposely planted to stand close to the partially eroded stone walls, the homes of our fore-fathers, forgotten foundations of a people and a time. Ride with your eyes open; the botanical names of flower, tree, bush and shrub won't be needed to bring you the spirit-exhilarating beauty of the Spring about you. Lilacs, blue-red and brilliant; flowering dogwood imported long ago from the hedges of England, a mass of lovely, cream-white flowers; violets; small, pale lavender of surpassing fragrance. Everywhere, the bell-shaped blossoms of the forsythia that found its way out of China and is now a bright glowing piece of the pattern out of which Putnam Valley's landscape emerges to gladden your heart.

And then, if you have decided to make Moonlight Ridge the turning point of your first Spring ride, you'll trot by several more old houses. The earth comprising their site will be upturned, ready for seed already planted to yield the annual crop of corn, tomatoes, greens and such, sustenance for the family and their cows, horses, goat and the ever present chickens. The puppies that yipped at your horse's hooves or who ran out senselessly, as puppies will, underneath his very nose, will be gangly-growth, just as carefree and just as heedless. Up on Moonlight Ridge, you, your horse and all Life itself will be one gladdened combination. On the Ridge, the grasses will be blowing like undulating waves of a pale yellow ocean. The trails taking you far up
and deep down, will be a veritable shower of blossoms. In one or two really favored spots, dewy lilies of the valley will lie in close beds at your feet. From the Ride's summit, the Hudson River will shimmer below you in the sunlight-a blue, bright reflection of the new-born sky above.

So, if you are Winter-weary-sing with me as we ride along:

Oh, give me days, lots of days
Up at Cimarron I love,
Don't fence me in.
Let me ride those old trails under sunny
 Skies above.
But don't fence me in.

Let me find at the Ranch all the gang
I long for
Down in the barn, just the horse I
Mourn for
Send me up to Cimarron, the Ranch
I'm strong for
Don't fence me in.

Just turn me loose, let me straddle a
Stock saddle
Underneath blue Putnam skies
On my Cayuse let me wander over yonder
'till I see the Catskills rise,
I want to turn my back on trouble and
Sadness
Go where life offers only gladness
Can't stand the city and it's endless
Madness,
Don't fence me in!

~Robin Snyder

Staghorn, of Course

Remember the Front Lawn

Ready & Waiting for You

We are still dancing

The Good Old Days...

- 202 -

Robin has described CIMARRON so well that, truly, I feel anything I might add to her description would indeed be superfluous.

She has put into words exactly what I knew was here... and never did get the time to notice, but I know so many of you have noticed it, have seen it, and now will feel it "pull" you so that may experience it again.

And so ... are you ready for FUN at CIMARRON? We are ready and waiting to see you get it!

The horses are in fine fettle; one could not find a better string of Western saddle horses anyplace! Under the capable care of our own Mike Hastings and Joe Brennan they are ready and willing to take you along the never-to-be forgotten trails.

We are happy to tell you, too, that Bill is coming back to cook for us ... and you will know that, as far as the food is concerned. It will be PAR EXCELLENCE!

I want to thank you for your loyal support of Cimarron in Vern's absence, And I don't have to tell you how happy it has made him!

Do you know that our own Jim Gunther is now PRIVATE JIM GUNTHER? He said goodbye to Civilian Life on the 26th of February, and while all of us who love him were very sad, we are certainly proud of him.... Proud because he insisted on enlisting even though they refused to give him a release from his essential and important war job. Jim felt that he just could not go on living with an easy berth when so many other men are sacrificing their lives! Aren't you proud of Cimarron's own Jim?

We are proud, too, of Margie Anderson whom most of you surely remember. She has enlisted in the Red Cross and expects to go overseas. We will miss her. Betty Pierson gave her a farewell party at the Belmont Plaza Hotel in New York recently. Betty and I attended and we certainly had a wonderful time... laughing just every minute of course, at ... guess who? ... Harry Crofford!

We surprised them all by bringing Jimmie Eickler along who is home on a 30 day furlough after many months overseas. Jimmie looks SO well... my goodness is he handsome in a uniform! ... and all he talks about is the day when he can come home to CIMARRON and ride the trails once more!

I don't like to introduce a sad note into this letter, but we just learned that Bob Berry is "Missing in Action" and we thought we would let you know about it.

Bob married Frances Motta, you know, and Frances has been quite ill ever since the receipt of the bad news. We hope and pray that he will be found and he is all right.

Grace and Gene have a son ... born on St. Valentine...s Day... and they have named him Vern Michael... "Vern" for Vern, and "Michael" for Mike. Grace and Gene met at Cimarron and were married at Cimarron. When I read for whom they named the baby, I got a big lump in my throat! I know that Vern will be mighty proud of the news!

And so our plans for you enjoyment and entertainment this coming season are ready... and we hope to continue with the usual Sunday Rodeos with our own Mike Hastings as arena director. At this time I want to say that we are grateful to Frank Steinrock for his announcing of our radios whenever he was here... his introduction and description of the different events always made our blood run faster with excitement and anticipation ... and in more ways than one Frank has helped me with the responsibility of the ranch... His suggestions and help, so willingly and generously given, have made CIMARRON a better place to live in, in many ways, and they will long be remembered.

For those of you who remember Vern and may be wondering where he is and how he is, may I tell you that our Big Boss is in Germany now, with the First Army, going through the toughest part of it all with them all. He writes that they are playing their "return engagement" after being pushed back in the German Offensive in December, when Vern's division was almost completely wiped out! That everything is so encouraging on every front and he is certain we are in the final days, and certainly weeks of the war...so...MAYBE HE WILL BE HOME SOON, HUH? And Doc is close to him going through the same thing with him... Doc says he doesn't know how anyone can live through such hell... but they are Cimarron's heros ... and now Jim has joined them. God bless them all!

NOTICE!

Arrangements made with "Rodeo Fans of America" Magazine.

Cimarron Ranch has bought a page of this monthly publication, and each month our "Mail Pouch" will be on one of it's pages... giving you all the news, announcements, etc. of Cimarron. A subscription to this magazine is $1.50 per year. If you would like to have one, would you kindly let me know, and send your check to me here at Cimarron? ... Please draw the check to the order of RODEO FANS OF AMERICA. Thank You, Lu Walter

Cimarron

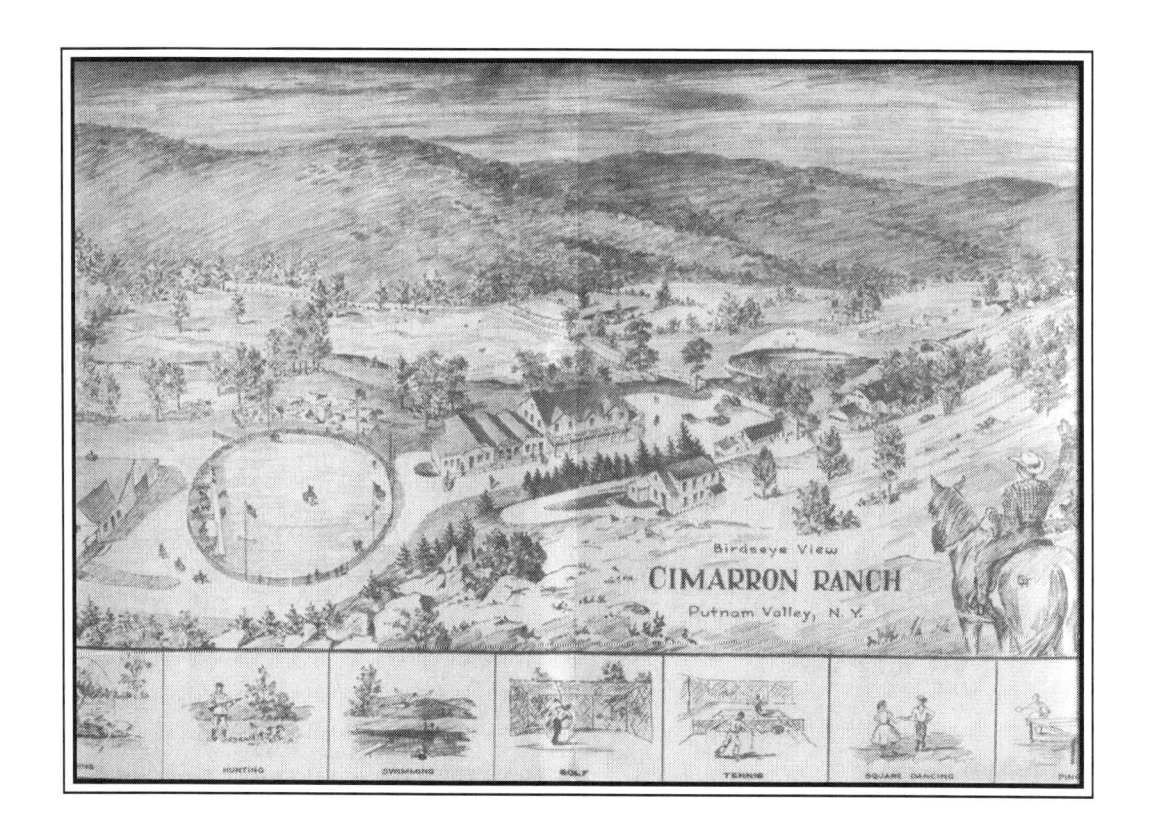

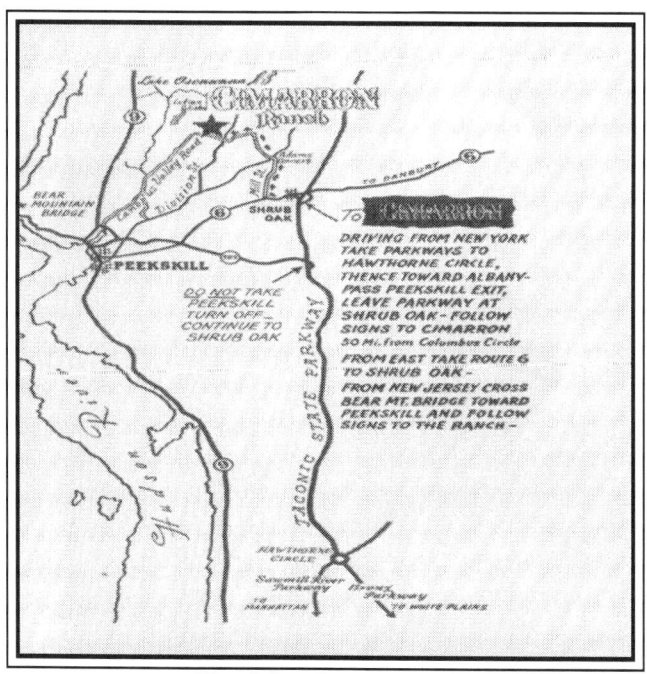

**Hand sketched cover of
Stationary from
Cimarron Ranch**

- 205 -

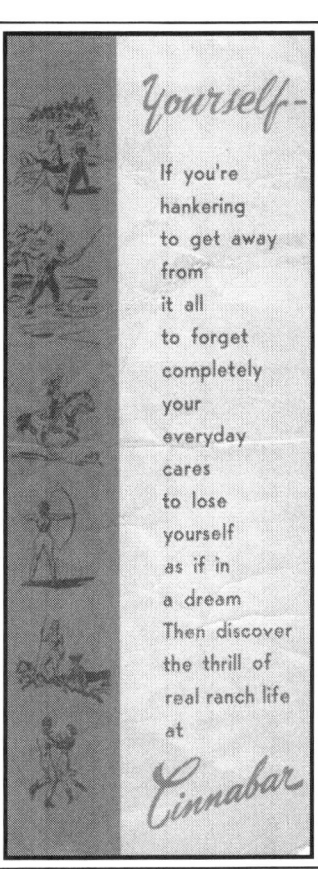

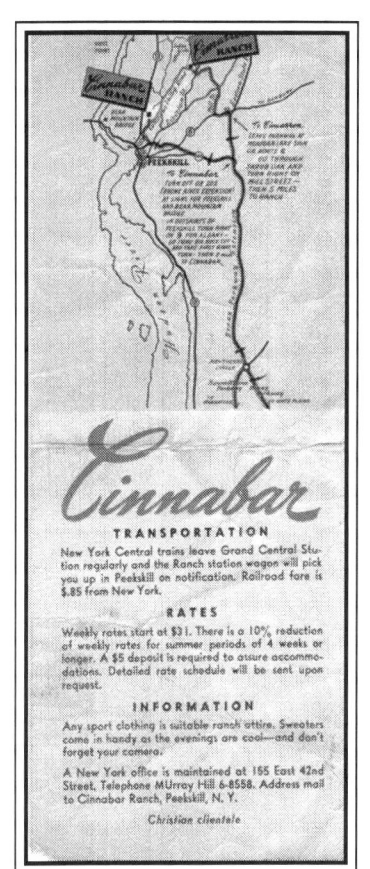

Placemat from Cimarron Ranch

CIMARRON Dude Ranch

WESTERNTOWN, AT CIMARRON RANCH
IN PUTNAM VALLEY, NEW YORK

Only 50 miles from Columbus Circle

In the rugged hill section of Putnam County

The Old West Transported to the East

In the heart of a cool, primitive woodland, in a land rich in the lore of the Revolution, sets Cimarron Ranch—the most authentically-Western of all dude ranches in the East. Cimarron is famous for its replica of a real Western cow-country town, built along a dirt street, separating the barns and rodeo arena from the main ranch quarters. Built to perpetuate and preserve the flavor of the Old West, it provides a focal point for the lighter side of life with its dummy Sheriff's office; the Last Chance Saloon, for your favorite beverages before dinner; the Silver Saddle Trading Post, selling ranch togs and Western souvenirs; the Round-Up Café for a snack, coffee or ice cream; and the Powder River Hotel where the Saturday night and midweek Square Dances are held. Westerntown, reminiscent of Abilene or Dodge City in their hey-days, is a page from the past for today's pleasure.

Ride on Western-bred and Western-trained Saddle Horses

There are slow rides with instructions for the beginner—intermediate rides for the more advanced—and, of course, regular rides for "old hands" who know their Western riding.

Since ranch life is the very essence of informality, dress accordingly. Sports clothes are ideal.

While riding is tops on the list of sports at Cimarron, there are a multitude of other diversions for your pleasure—Swimming, Tennis, Fishing, Hiking, Shooting, Archery, Badminton, Horseshoe Pitching, Baseball, Ping-pong, Movies, Parties, Games, Dancing, Picnics, Breakfast Rides and Rodeos. Time never drags at Cimarron. The Sunday morning ride to Mass at Graymoor is a ranch feature!

Ranch life is topped off with a moonlight hayride.

JOIN THE FUN!

Open from May to November

Special programs are arranged for the holiday week-ends and a
Halloween Masquerade Party with prizes for the cleverest
costumes, is one of the highlights of the year.
Pre-Season and late Fall, unlimited horseback riding
is provided whenever possible.

Mail address: Putnam Valley, N. Y. Railroad and telegraph: Peekskill, N. Y.
Direct N. Y. C. phone: Lorraine 2-7777

A sparkling clear pond of cool mountain spring water, right in the ranch front yard, is the natural swimming pool for Cimarron guests. Its white sand beach is grand for sunning.

Special emphasis is placed on horseback riding instructions, assuring even the beginner the "know-how" of riding.

Once a week, during July and August, the arena comes to life with a full-scale rodeo in which Cimarron guests participate, together with nationally known rodeo stars.

Come and Get It!

When the dinner bell rings at Cimarron, the table groans under its load of wholesome American dishes...from hearty Western beef stew to the finest roast prime ribs of beef...the fresh hot bread in the morning, the pies and cakes at supper time.

THE ENTERTAINMENT PROGRAM AT CIMARRON IS FLEXIBLE

Resident orchestras provide gay tunes in the evening for social and square dancing. Square your sets and ALL join in!

Cowboy musicians give forth with background music for group "sings".

Arena games and rodeo practice are usual during twilight hours.

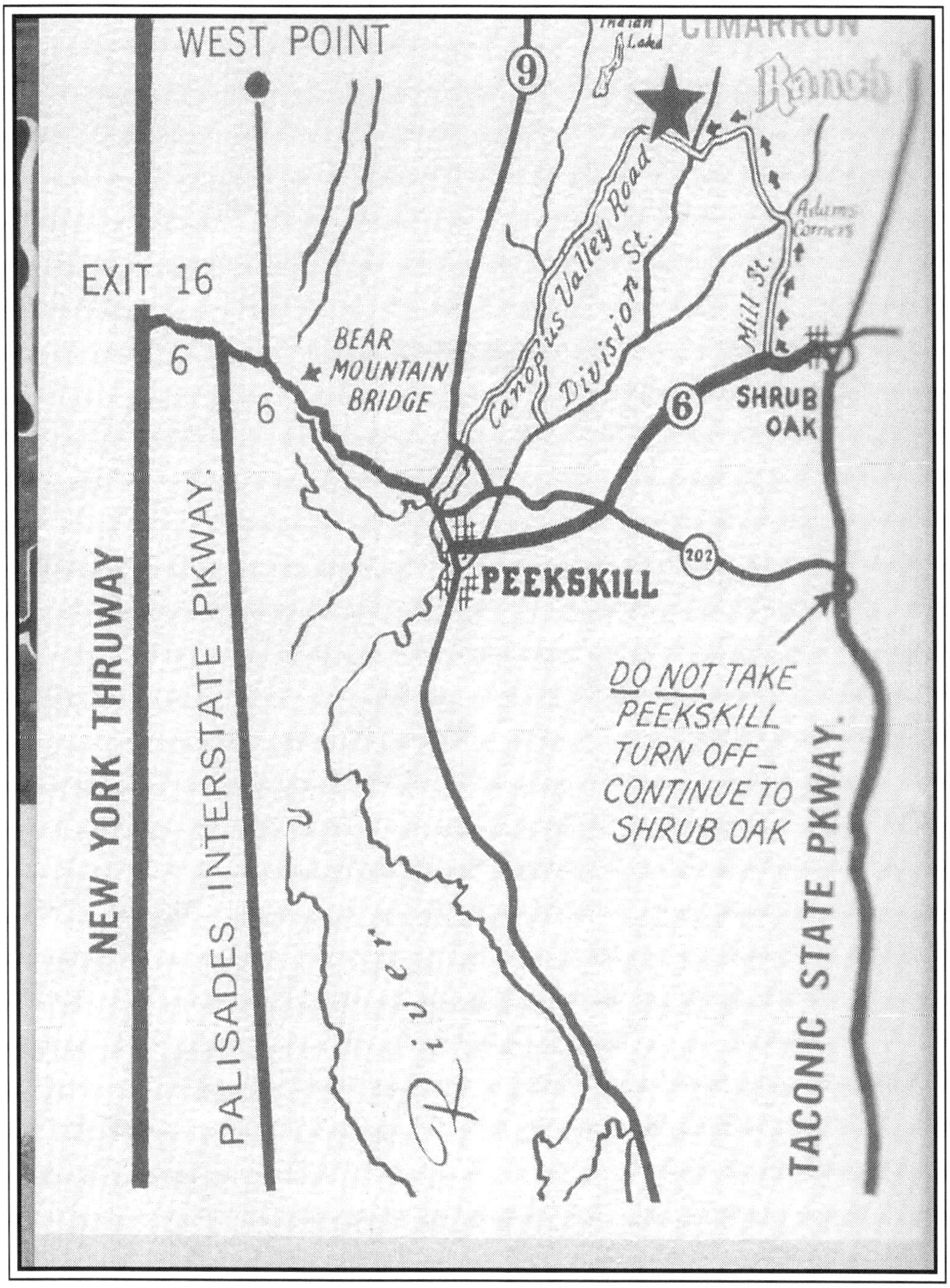

WEST POINT
9
Indian Lake
CIMARRON
Ranch
Adams Corners
Canopus Valley Road
Division St.
Mill St.
EXIT 16
6
6
BEAR MOUNTAIN BRIDGE
6
SHRUB OAK
PEEKSKILL
202
DO NOT TAKE PEEKSKILL TURN OFF_ CONTINUE TO SHRUB OAK
NEW YORK THRUWAY
PALISADES INTERSTATE PKWAY.
River
TACONIC STATE PKWAY.

> This wish for a "mighty fine Christmas"
> And a New Year along the same line
> Is coming today to some people
> Who certainly are mighty fine!
>
> *Cimarron Ranch*

Vern Walter, Lu Walter, C.J. Walter, Allan Walter, Bob Lehman, Peggy Walter, Stanley Walter, 2 unknown kitchen help, Art Prichard, Jim Gunther, Doc and Fred Dasher

Christmas card from Cimarron Ranch Owners and Ranch Hands

Cinnabar Christmas Card

CIMARRON Ranch NEWSLETTER

SPRING 1996   **NO. 4**

CIMARRON REUNION '95
by Betty H. Bickler

Dick & Debbie Tarrantino gave us a really warm welcome. Dave O'Halloran arranged for us to have a private dining and hospitality room. To top it off, he brought up Joe Phillips, Smokey, and his dogs to put on his great show. The International Police Assoc. from Baltimore were there and it was just like being at Cimarron. They entertained us with the latest line-dancing and we showed them how to square dance-a la Cimarron. This group will be there when we hold the '96 Reunion at Pinegrove, Sept. 13, 14, and 15, 1996. Dave will send out brochures in July. Get them back to Pinegrove. Mark it on your calendar, NOW! We know everyone can't make it every year, but some of us won't make it in 5 years. Milly Pritchard called and gave me the sad news that Artie had died in May. He was one of the GREATEST CALLERS, I have ever heard. Val Young and Earl Walters have also crossed over that great divide.

REUNION SET FOR SEPT 13-14-15, 1996

SADDLE UP FOR THE CIMARRON RANCH REUNION WEEKEND. IT'S GOING TO BE A REAL 'BLAST' AT THE PINEGROVE RANCH, KERHONKSON N.Y.

SEPTEMBER 13-14-15-1996 WE WILL GET A "TASTE OF THE WEST." RIDING*SQUARE DANCING*HAYRIDES*TENNIS*GOLF*PING-PONG*BOCCI*GREAT FOOD AND ACCOMMODATIONS. DICK TARRANTINO PROMISES A SPECIAL 'HOSPITALITY ROOM'.

MARK LEWIS

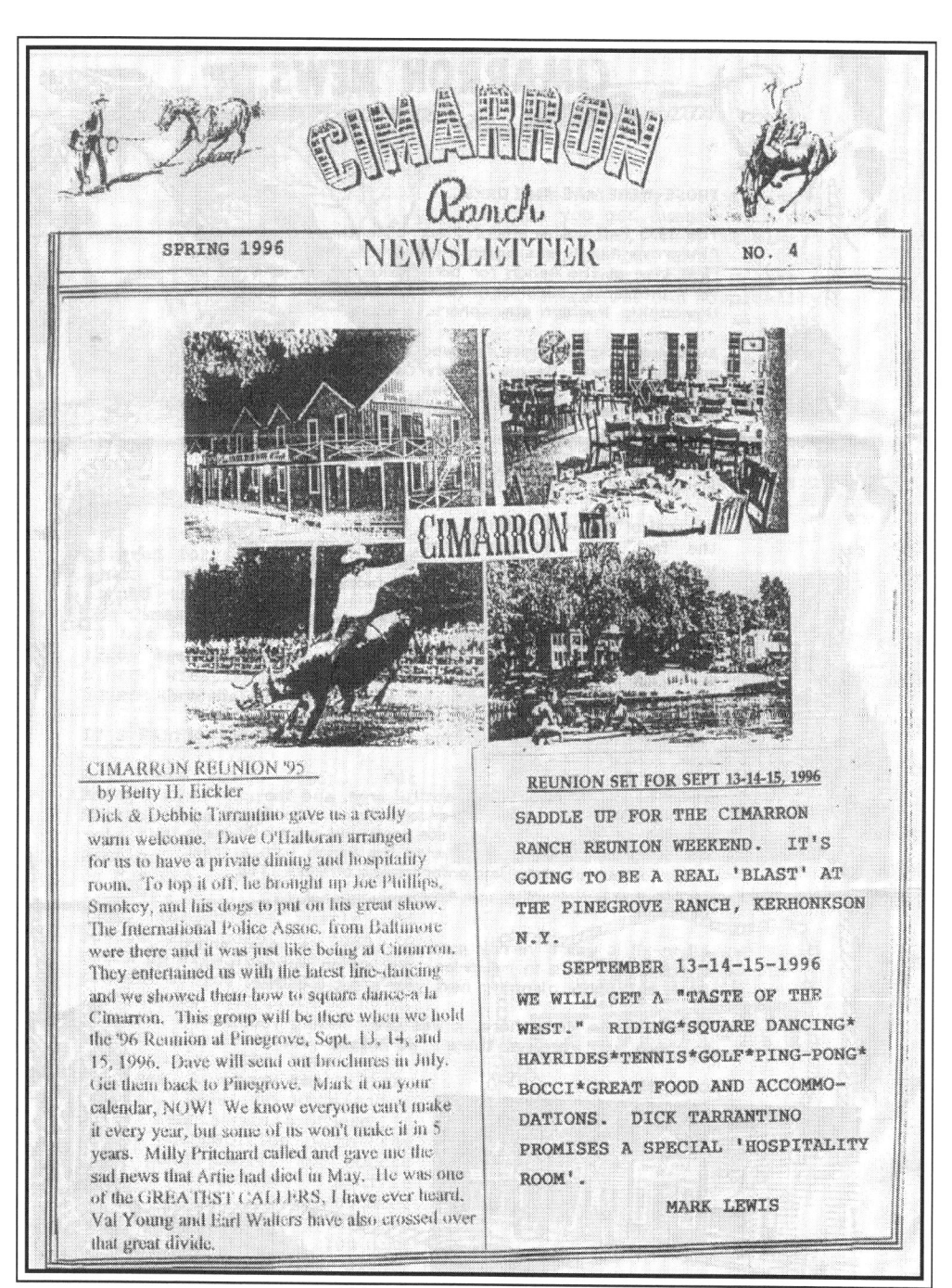

1996 – The fans still gather

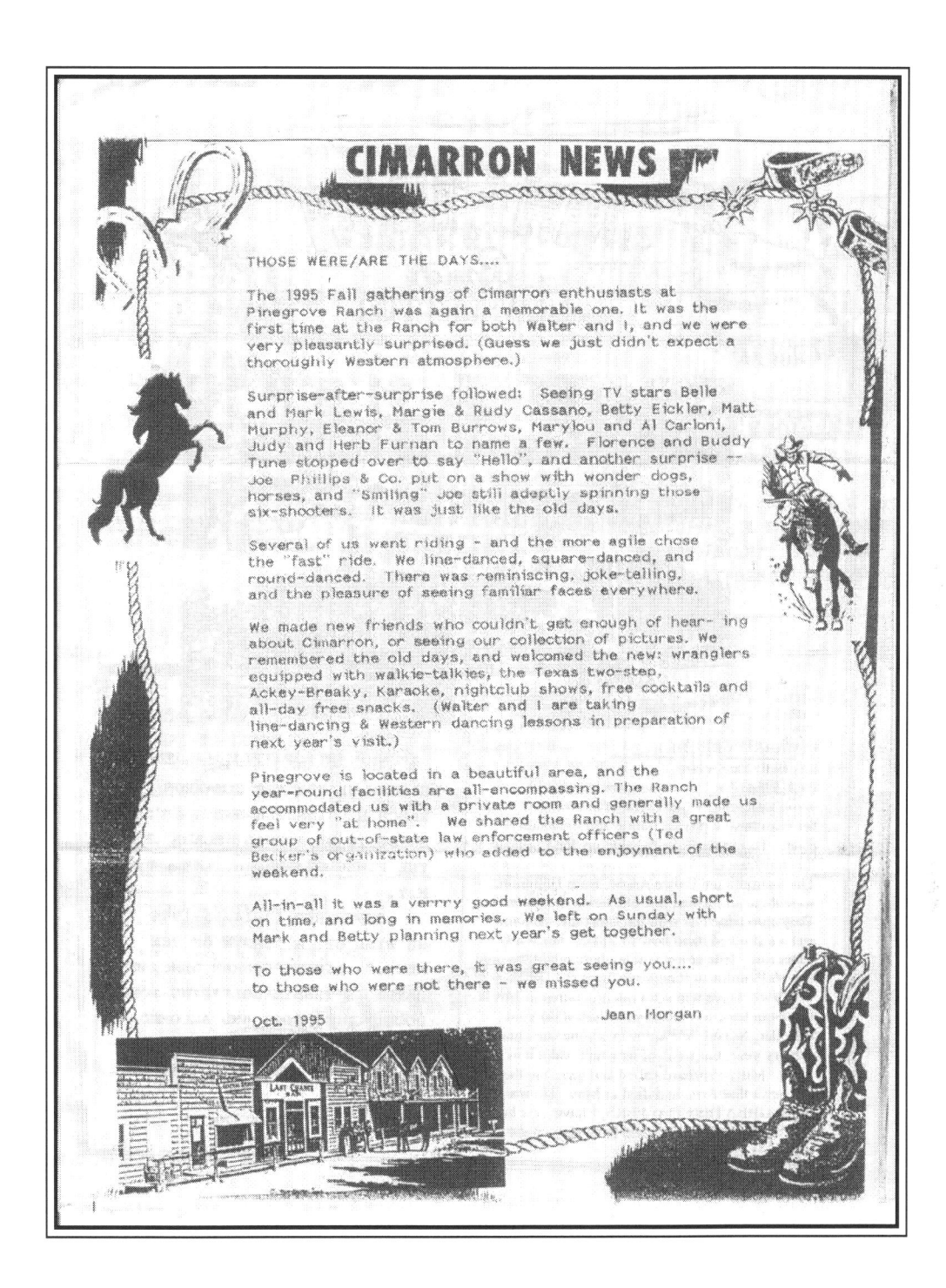

CIMARRON NEWS

THOSE WERE/ARE THE DAYS....

The 1995 Fall gathering of Cimarron enthusiasts at Pinegrove Ranch was again a memorable one. It was the first time at the Ranch for both Walter and I, and we were very pleasantly surprised. (Guess we just didn't expect a thoroughly Western atmosphere.)

Surprise-after-surprise followed: Seeing TV stars Belle and Mark Lewis, Margie & Rudy Cassano, Betty Eickler, Matt Murphy, Eleanor & Tom Burrows, Marylou and Al Carloni, Judy and Herb Furnan to name a few. Florence and Buddy Tune stopped over to say "Hello", and another surprise -- Joe Phillips & Co. put on a show with wonder dogs, horses, and "Smiling" Joe still adeptly spinning those six-shooters. It was just like the old days.

Several of us went riding - and the more agile chose the "fast" ride. We line-danced, square-danced, and round-danced. There was reminiscing, joke-telling, and the pleasure of seeing familiar faces everywhere.

We made new friends who couldn't get enough of hear- ing about Cimarron, or seeing our collection of pictures. We remembered the old days, and welcomed the new: wranglers equipped with walkie-talkies, the Texas two-step, Ackey-Breaky, Karaoke, nightclub shows, free cocktails and all-day free snacks. (Walter and I are taking line-dancing & Western dancing lessons in preparation of next year's visit.)

Pinegrove is located in a beautiful area, and the year-round facilities are all-encompassing. The Ranch accommodated us with a private room and generally made us feel very "at home". We shared the Ranch with a great group of out-of-state law enforcement officers (Ted Becker's organization) who added to the enjoyment of the weekend.

All-in-all it was a verrry good weekend. As usual, short on time, and long in memories. We left on Sunday with Mark and Betty planning next year's get together.

To those who were there, it was great seeing you.... to those who were not there - we missed you.

Oct. 1995   Jean Morgan

CIMARRON ROUNDUP

THE CIMARRON LEGEND: OLD MIKE

CIMARRON PROFILE

"Old Mike Hastings" known and beloved for many years by the Rodeo Cowboys, Mike Hastings earned the tribute of having the Cimarron Rodeo Arena named in his honor. Mike held the 1928 World Championship in steer wrestling in Madison Square Garden.

IT'S PARTY TIME!

Well here we go again. **Get Ready!** Give yourself a break. **Set the date.** We are ready to join the Great "Cimarron Ranch Reunion" once again. This will be our 8th time around. Don't miss the fun. Throw on your duds, forget the hustle and bustle and come on down to catch up with all your past and present riding friends. We can promise you that there is never a dull moment. It's just wonderful to see familiar faces and reminisce the good times. Needless to say that Dick, Deborah, Dave and Nick and I enjoy tennis while there is always competition with the ping pong table, or boccie ball, horseshoes, shuffle board, archery, indoor/outdoor swimming, basketball courts and of course the **HORSES**. You name it and there is always plenty to keep you busy. If for some reason you get hungry with all this exercise, there is always free snack bar from 10:00AM till midnight, plus cocktail parties and our own hospitality room. What more can one ask for?? It's fun to see that there are now three (3) generations enjoying the reunion and experiencing the days of way back then. So pack up the grandchildren and show them how we get back in the saddle again. Looking forward to seeing you all there...
Nick and Jean Stella

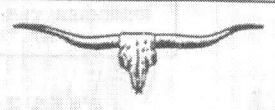

- 216 -

REMEMBER THE DATES SEPT. 13-14-15, 1996
AT THE PINEGROVE

CIMARRON NEWS

FROM THE MAILBAG...
by Betty H. Eickler

Letters--we get letters, but not enough of them. We send the newsletter out to 189, but only hear from about 5. So let us know how you're doing. Ted Becker is still traveling all over the globe. This time he took his Grandson, Jason, to London. The Bobby (policeman) gave Jason the honor of riding his 17 hand horse. Was he thrilled. He also has a new granddaughter. Heard from Ceal Geary, who keeps busy dog showing. She sent a card of her two Pugs. Good luck with the showing. Lee & Frank Catandella sent Mark & I a long chatty letter. They have 8 grandchildren & 2 are in College. Dick & Jane Borden from Las Vegas also write. I have a new horse, Dork, a gray that's over 16 hands high--I need a step ladder to get on him--when I'm, which isn't often. I went to England, Scotland, Wales, Canary Islands (rode a camel there), New Orleans, Cancun, and the Grand Caymans. I hope to see Ted Becker when I pass thru Jackson Hole this summer. That's all the space I get--so let us hear from you all.

FOR RESERVATIONS OR INFO CALL:
MARK LEWIS (914) 564-6864
BETTY EICKLER 255-1902
DAVE O'HALLORAN (PINEGROVE)
1-800-346-4626

EMPTY SADDLES:
WE WERE SADDENED & SHOCKED TO LEARN OF THE PASSING OF GOOD FRIENDS. VAL YOUNG ARTIE PRITCHARD AND EARL WALTERS.

Editor's Note

PLEASE SEND US YOUR NEWS ITEMS AS IT PERTAINS TO OUR CIMARRON RANCH FRIENDS RODEOS, EVENTS, ETC. FOR FUTURE ISSUES OF OUR NEWSLETTER.

CIMARRON ROUND-UP
NEWSLETTER
124 Ridge Rd.
Montgomery, NY 12549

MARK LEWIS ....EDITOR
CONTRIBUTORS
BETTY EICKLER*JUDY FURMAN
JEAN MORGAN*BELLE LEWIS
JEAN & NICK STELLA

CIMARRON ROUND-UP
NEWSLETTER
124 Ridge Rd.
Montgomery, N.Y. 12549

NEWSLETTER

CIMARRON INDEX TO FUN

I NTRODUCTION
M ILES FROM N.Y.C. – SEASON
A CTIVITIES – CLOTHES
R ATES – ACCOMMODATIONS
R EAL WESTERNTOWN
O UR RANCH PERSONNEL
N OVICE RIDER INSTRUCTION

Fifty years ago, the pioneer Western ranchers offered their Eastern friends and relatives, open ranch riding and simple ranch fare for their entertainment. It was so completely satisfying, such an exhilarating way of life, that their visitors insisted on paying for their stay, to feel free to return for their annual vacations. The city clothes and tenderfoot ways of the visitors earned them the humorous term "dudes" . . . and thus was born "dude ranching."

Vern Walter, son of a Western pioneer, came East in the late twenties to realize his boyhood ambition, to be a traveling salesman. Eventually, he conceived the idea of providing Easterners, lacking the time for long-distance travel, this popular, carefree Western way of life, and opened the first Eastern dude ranch in 1930. The broad experience and many acquaintances gained thru traveling the breadth of the United States, living in Canada, visits to Old Mexico, and Service in the European Theatre during the last War, ideally qualify him to operate one of America's finest guest ranches.

I NTRODUCTION
M ILES FROM N.Y.C. – SEASON
A CTIVITIES – CLOTHES
R ATES – ACCOMMODATIONS
R EAL WESTERNTOWN
O UR RANCH PERSONNEL
N OVICE RIDER INSTRUCTION

SEASON

CIMARRON is open from April to December. Guests are accommodated for Easter Week and weekends only in April ... full time from May thru October ... and then for weekends only in November. Special programmes are arranged for the holiday weekends and a Halloween Masquerade Party, with prizes for the cleverest costumes, is one of the highlights of the year. Pre-Season and late Fall unlimited horseback riding is provided whenever possible.

* *

CIMARRON RANCH is situated fifty miles north of New York City, in an area called "The Hudson Highlands," due East of West Point, South of Fahnestock State Park, six miles West of Taconic State Parkway (which affords quick access to and from New York City by motor), eight miles North of Peekskill, on the main line of the New York Central Railroad where guests arriving by train are met upon notification, at no charge, and only a little over an hour from New York City, yet in a seemingly new World. Breezes over the Taconic Mountain Range cool the summer sun-rays and dispel the city's high humidity. Your weather man refers to the area as "the normally cooler Northern suburbs."

M ILES FROM N.Y.C. — SEASON
A CTIVITIES — CLOTHES
R ATES — ACCOMMODATIONS
R EAL WESTERNTOWN
O UR RANCH PERSONNEL
N OVICE RIDER INSTRUCTION

RANCH WEAR

Ranch life is the very essence of informality and you dress accordingly. Sports clothes are ideal for rest, relaxation and fun. For riding, we recommend old-fashioned light-weight longies that reach to the ankle, blue jeans, a plaid shirt and cowboy boots to protect your ankles, a ten-gallon hat and gay kerchief for camera effect, and a jacket for the cool of the evening. We have transparent cover-all capes that can be tied on the saddle for your protection in the event of rain. And, don't forget your camera and lots of film!

* *

While horseback riding is the number one sport at the ranch, it is closely followed by the water sports in our clear, cool pool, which is right in the ranch front yard. There is a new electric-powered roto-wheel for your fun, and a white sand beach for sunbathing. There is also tennis, fishing, hiking, shooting, archery, badminton, horseshoe pitching, baseball, ping-pong, movies, parties, games, square dances, hay-rides, picnics, breakfast rides, and a regular rodeo with guest games, followed by a real Western barbecue, every Sunday during July and August. Time never drags ... all you have to do is join the fun!

The Sunday morning horseback ride to Mass at GRAYMOOR is an event long to be remembered.

A CTIVITIES — CLOTHES
R ATES — ACCOMMODATIONS
R EAL WESTERNTOWN
O UR RANCH PERSONNEL
N OVICE RIDER INSTRUCTION

There are several choices of accommodations... first GD—*Girls' Dormitories* — MB—*Men's Bunkhouses*... which are rooms with two or three double-deck twin-size beds with inner-spring mattresses. Second, NB—*Double or Twin-Bedded Rooms* with convenient baths in the hall. Third, CB—*Rooms With Connecting Bath* (2 rooms share one bathroom). Fourth, WB—*Rooms With Private Bath* have combination tub and shower baths. All rooms are for double occupancy, and when a room is reserved for single occupancy, there is a slight additional charge.

The food is the finest money can buy, skillfully prepared by competent chefs in clean, modern kitchens, and served on platters, ranch-style. There is a weekly breakfast, picnic lunch and Western-style barbecue served in the open.

The week-day rates, including your room, meals, horseback riding and instructions, all sports and entertainment, with transportation to church and the railroad station, start at $11.00 per day for the girls' dormitories and men's bunkhouses ... and are $1.00 more for each better-type accommodation. The Weekday Special of five weekdays is $1.00 per day less. Weekends, from Friday PM to Sunday PM cost approximately three weekdays. Weekly rates are approximately seven times the daily rate. SUNDOWN COTTAGE ACCOMMODATIONS are $1.00 per day less due to the distance "one quarter mile from the main ranch buildings." In July and August, Sundown Cottage will be used to accommodate children and they have a separate programme which does not conflict with the adult schedule.

R ATES – ACCOMMODATIONS
R EAL WESTERNTOWN
O UR RANCH PERSONNEL
N OVICE RIDER INSTRUCTION

The Still of the Night Enfolds Western Town Street but there is a Gay Crowd Inside Singing, Dancing and Making Merry.

OUT WEST

CIMARRON is famous for its real Western Town, built along a dirt street, separating the barns and rodeo arena from the main ranch buildings. It is the center of much ranch activity and consists of a dummy Sheriff's Office; the Silver Saddle Trading Post, selling ranch togs and Western souvenirs; the Last Chance Saloon, for your favorite cocktail before dinner; the Round-Up Cafe for a late snack, Mexican enchiladas, or chile, charcoal-broiled steaks, or coffee and ice cream at any time; and the POWDER RIVER HOTEL where the Saturday night square-dances and mid-week magic shows are held.

R EAL WESTERNTOWN
O UR RANCH PERSONNEL
N OVICE RIDER INSTRUCTION

Regardless of location, the basic requirements for a dude ranch are . . . to be rurally situated; to provide ample riding trails thru interesting terrain; offer comfortable living quarters for guests; serve ample, appetizing food for healthy, outdoor appetites; provide swimming facilities and have other recreational activities, plus an evening entertainment programme to round out the day. However, the outstanding character of any dude ranch is its personality, which is reflected by the management and its staff.

CIMARRON offers, besides Vern Walter, owner-manager . . .

LU WALTER, Brooklyn-born wife of the owner, who supervises your living comfort, and selects your compatible vacation guests . . .

JIM GUNTER, joint owner, who supervises the working operation of CIMARRON and its staff of approximately 40 employees . . .

BETTY GARRAMONE, who joined CIMARRON ten years ago, is the ranch-treasurer, and is married to our popular manager of Western Town . . .

FRANK GARRAMONE, old-time CIMARRON guest, who is well qualified to run Western Town, from the experience gained operating his own supper club . . .

MIKE HASTINGS, World-famous Cowboy, one of the few remaining real cowboys of the Old West, who has charge of CIMARRON'S riding and rodeo stock . . .

BILL GALLICK, CIMARRON'S Chef for the past ten years, who learned his trade on the Santa Fe Super Chief under the supervision of Fred Harvey . . .

SYLVIA NOEL, who has operated CIMARRON'S Silver Saddle Trading Post for six years, and who has truly become a part of CIMARRON.

OLLIE FLANNER, long a part of CIMARRON, who is at your beck and call in the ROUND-UP CAFE, for early coffee call or a late snack . . .

RAY CIVERCHIA, whose smiling countenance is always a welcome sign in the Last Chance Saloon . . .

MARK AND NENA BARKER, of Arizona, who are not exactly new to CIMARRON. They headed our entertainment program in 1949 . . .

AND you'll meet many others, all anxious to serve your needs . . . a real guarantee that your vacation will be a pleasant one.

O UR RANCH PERSONNEL

N OVICE RIDER INSTRUCTION

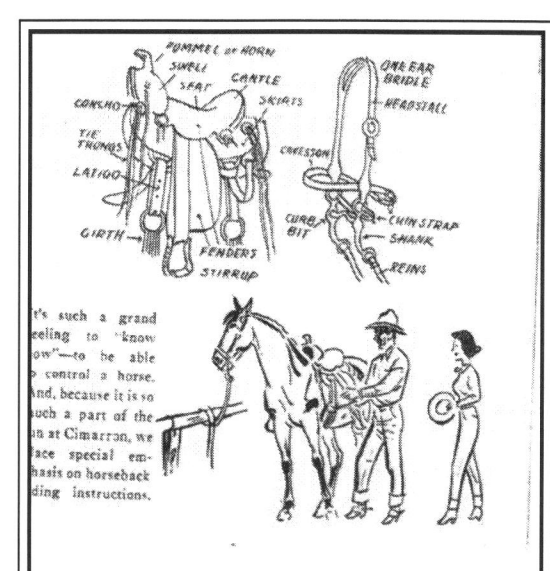

It's such a grand feeling to "know how"—to be able to control a horse. And, because it is so much a part of the fun at Cimarron, we place special emphasis on horseback riding instructions.

RIDING LESSONS

There are three riding groups at CIMARRON . . . beginners, slow and regular. If you are learning to ride, you will be given a book which details the basic principles of horseback riding, then practice on a mechanical horse, before you are given your first mount. Then you are taken into the rodeo arena to learn to sit the different gaits of a horse, and how to control him. When you have acquired sufficient confidence, you are taken for a short trail ride, and usually, within a week, you will have progressed thru the slow stage and be able to join the regular group.

N OVICE RIDER INSTRUCTION

C.J. Walter and Allan at Cinnabar Ranch in ad for 1941 Dodge

New York Times – 1942
Dude Ranch Ads

A THREE-HOUR RIDE—LEAVING RANCH BUILDINGS   A REGULAR SUNDAY FEATURE—"THE RODEO"

CINNABAR RANCH
3000 ACRES OF WONDEROUS COUNTRY 1 HR FROM NEW YORK
PEEKSKILL 402
The Ranchiest Ranch in the East

OCTOBER AND NOVEMBER ARE TWO OF THE BEST MONTHS AT CINNABAR . . . BRISK THREE-HOUR RIDES MORNING AND AFTERNOON . . . THRU GLORIOUS TRAILS THAT ARE AT THEIR HEIGHT IN AUTUMN BEAUTY.

Do You Know

- That thousands of people acclaim Cinnabar as a touch of the Rockies right near New York City.

- That the "C. J. Walters" make you feel right at home, and their congeniality is soon spread among the guests.

- That Cinnabar is known for their young, carefree, fun-loving "dudes."

- That Cinnabar boasts of 126 horses — which are the finest saddle and rodeo stock east of the Rockies.

- That Cinnabar's two beautiful lakes afford pleasure both summer and winter.

- That rodeos, square dances, hay rides, barbeques, are all regular ranch features.

Also—

- That Cinnabar's rooms are comfortably heated and tastefully furnished.

- That we serve good wholesome American food — and plenty of it.

- That hundreds of Cinnabar romances have resulted in happy marriages.

- That there are fast and frequent trains to and from N.Y.C. Our ranch car meets most trains.

- That rates begin at $50.00 per week, which include meals, lodging, and horseback riding every day.

- Our beautifully illustrated booklet will be sent you free upon request.

"CINNABAR'S LAKE CORRAL"

RIDING · RODEOS · SQUARE DANCES · HAY RIDES · LAKE SPORTS
MEMBER OF EASTERN DUDE RANCH ASSOCIATION—VISITORS WELCOME AT ALL TIMES

Spot Entertainment Magazine – October 1941

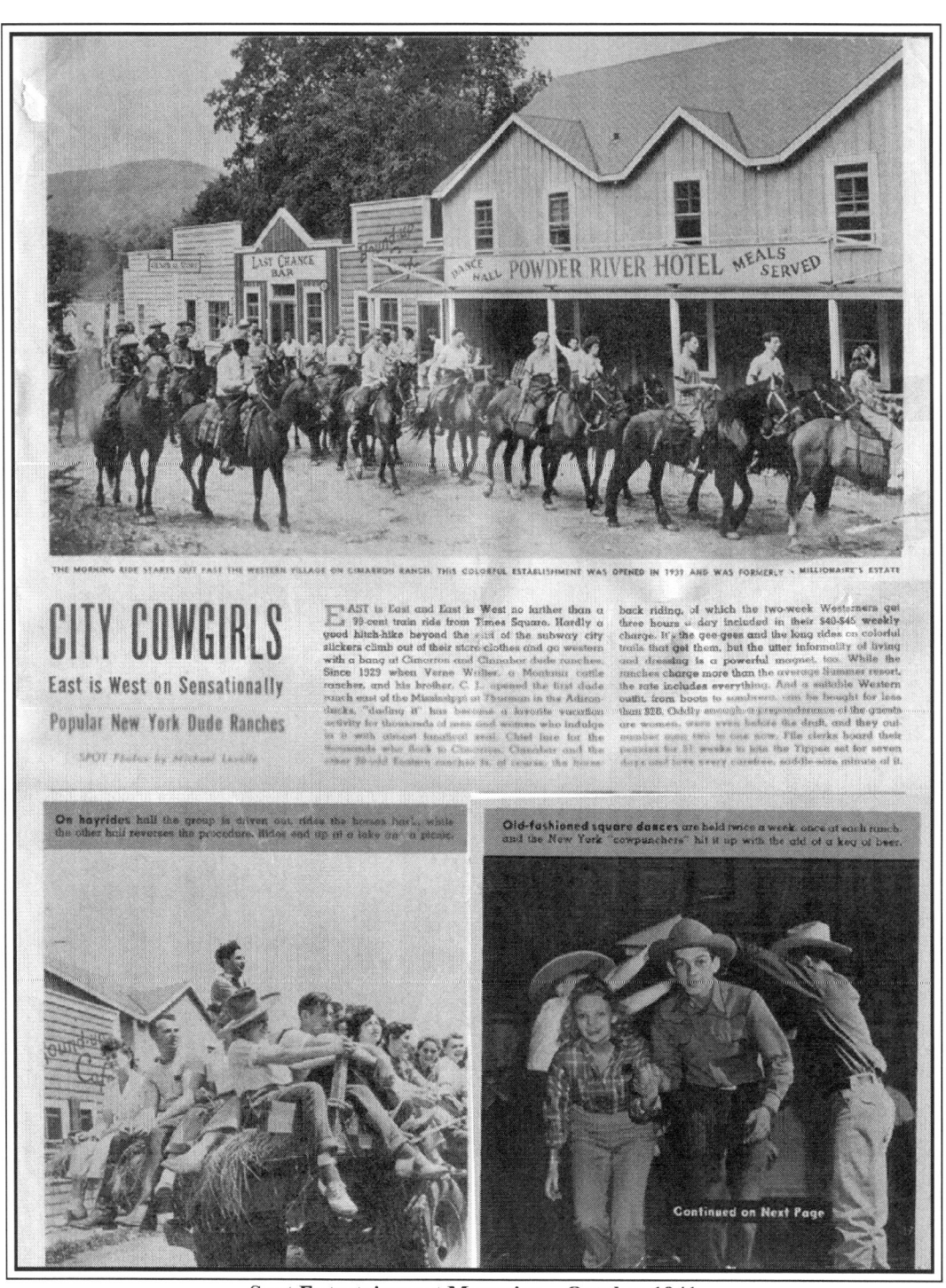

THE MORNING RIDE STARTS OUT PAST THE WESTERN VILLAGE ON CIMARRON RANCH. THIS COLORFUL ESTABLISHMENT WAS OPENED IN 1939 AND WAS FORMERLY A MILLIONAIRE'S ESTATE

CITY COWGIRLS

East is West on Sensationally Popular New York Dude Ranches

SPOT Photos by Michael Leville

EAST is East and East is West no further than a 99-cent train ride from Times Square. Hardly a good hitch-hike beyond the end of the subway city slickers climb out of their store-clothes and go western with a bang at Cimarron and Cinnabar dude ranches. Since 1929 when Verne Weller, a Montana cattle rancher, and his brother, C. J., opened the first dude ranch east of the Mississippi at Thurman in the Adirondacks, "duding it" has become a favorite vacation activity for thousands of men and women who indulge in it with almost fanatical zeal. Chief lure for the thousands who flock to Cimarron, Cinnabar and the other 30-odd Eastern ranches is, of course, the horseback riding, of which the two-week Westerners get three hours a day included in their $40-$45 weekly charge. It's the gee-gees and the long rides on colorful trails that get them, but the utter informality of living and dressing is a powerful magnet, too. While the ranches charge more than the average Summer resort, the rate includes everything. And a suitable Western outfit, from boots to sombrero, can be bought for less than $25. Oddly enough a preponderance of the guests are women, were even before the draft, and they outnumber men two to one now. File clerks hoard their pennies for 51 weeks to join the Yippee set for seven days and love every carefree, saddle-sore minute of it.

On hayrides half the group is driven out, rides the horses back, while the other half reverses the procedure. Rides end up at a lake or a picnic.

Old-fashioned square dances are held twice a week, once at each ranch, and the New York "cowpunchers" hit it up with the aid of a keg of beer.

Continued on Next Page

Spot Entertainment Magazine – October 1941

Spot Entertainment Magazine – October 1941

Spot Entertainment Magazine – October 1941

COUNTY FAIR PRINCIPALS—Here are some of the big shots in the Westchester County Fair. John M. Houston (center rear) is the general manager. Others in the picture, left to right, are: Back row: C. J. Walter, Jack Ready, Mr. Houston, Ruth Scripter and Jeff Price; middle row: Arleen Burtels, Alyce Walter and Dottie Walter; front row: Maxine Schwerd, Sue Craig and Peggie Ferrante.

"COPY, BOY!"

By Gene Ward

Peekskill, N. Y.—The dogwood blossoms blanket the hillsides just as they have every Spring since Hendrik Hudson sailed the Half Moon up this way; only this year they seem to have arrived earlier and bloomed more white and profuse than ever. And there's the rich pinkness of the wild cherry trees, the myriads of meadow and forest flowers, the winding trails and a good horse to make a man forget the troubles of the world for a little while. Old Mother Nature strokes you between the eyes and pretty soon the aches and pains go away.

That's why I came here to Cinnabar, the ranch of the Walter family in Putnam Valley, one tall hill view from the Hudson. Only 50 miles from New York City's confusion, it might well be 50 times 50 so complete is the transformation.

An old soldier once told me that heavy artillery fire had an effect on the weather, that after a severe bombardment there comes a hot, dry spell. Mebbe so. It has been hot and dry, but the guns booming on far-flung fronts have brought only peace and happiness here. And, like the guns, the dude ranching business is booming, the reservation list is more crowded than ever before with the names of those who want to forget, for a little while, so that they can go back to their jobs and carry on.

Some are soldiers. A few moments ago, one with a sergeant's chevrons on one arm and a pretty blonde on the other checked in and lanky Allen Walter, oldest son and the business boss of Cinnabar, has herded 'em off to the bunkhouse with their baggage.

Pretty soon Chef Charley will bang the luncheon gong and the soldier and his lass will go in to the long tables and meet the rest of the gang. After lunch the new albino colt, just three weeks old, will be shod and then, around 2:30, C. J. Allen's father and the corral boss of this here outfit, will have 'em up on horses. By dusk the sergeant and his gal will be hungrier and happier than they've been in a long, long time.

The Walter Family, Inc. (there are 13 of 'em including Vern, C. J.'s brother who operates nearby Cinnaron) certainly have an ideal site for their enterprise. Cinnabar is the old Stuyvesant Fish estate which once was run as a dairy farm and the countryside still talks of the workers who went around the big barns dressed in uniforms as spotless white as the creamy milk. The Walters' took over the estate three years ago and since have leased extra land so that, in all, they control 3,000 acres of woods, streams and trails. Every member of the family does a job and it works to perfection.

Newspaper Columnist Gene Ward's
"unbiased" article of Cinnabar Ranch!
Page 1

Stretching in front of the ranch proper—which is a cluster of eleven buildings, including the two huge barns which stable 75 horses in the peak Summer months—is a half-mile long lake which old Mr. Fish built at a cost of $110,000 in the hopes of selling it to a group of New York sportsmen. The lake is the only artificial touch to the whole set-up. All the rest is pure outdoors, a thick slice of the old west from corral to kitchen. The bunk houses are named after western states, everybody wears sombreros and gets blisters under their boots in the square dances at night. When you hit that hay, you're dead beat; when you're routed out early, the world is your oyster and all's right.

There are two rides a day, one in the morning and another in the afternoon. The group is divided up into a slow ride and a fast one, the first for the beginners. But even the best horsemen sometimes prefer the slow, lazy rides, for then they just sit in the saddle and absorb the fresh Spring that's in the green grass and the firm brown earth. Yesterday as we wended out way up over a small plateau I turned in the saddle to look back. C. J. saw me out of the corner of his eye.

"Makes quite a picture, eh, Gene?"

And it certainly did . . . the late sun slanting down on the long line of riders behind us, a line which stretched in and out of the trees and snaked on off down into the valley. There must have been 25 or 30 horses and riders in the string. The colors were so bright and the intervening shadows so deep and rich and the setting so right that I actually wished I had brushes and palette and could paint.

I think I'll always hold that picture in my mind. In fact, I'll never forget any moments of the past few days, probably because the contrast between war and peace has been so great. I'll never forget riding over to attend Mass at famous and beautiful Graymoor and the talk I had there with the young Franciscan friar. Or sitting on the porch as the moon came up and listening to Curly strumming and singing my favorites ... "You Are My Sunshine", ... "It Makes No Difference Now."

There goes that luncheon gong. And when you've been riding all morning food really means something. Hey, Chef, what's cookin'?

Newspaper Columnist Gene Ward's
"unbiased" article of Cinnabar Ranch!
Page 2

CINNABAR RANCH
PEEKSKILL, NEW YORK
Return Postage Guaranteed

CINNABAR DUDE RANCH NEWS

The Ranchiest Ranch in the East—Just like the West, Better Than the Rest.

1944   Peekskill, New York   Vol. IV, No. 1

Cinnabar's Rodeo Party Huge Success

Earl Walter bulldogging in one of our Weekly Rodeos

Our annual Rodeo party was held October 6th, 1943, at the Belvedere Hotel, and it was a big success. We had 330 guests and practically all were decked in Western togs. The rodeo show was the best of the 30 performances, so was thoroughly enjoyed by an enthusiastic crowd. The dance after the rodeo ended a gala evening. A group picture was taken at the Garden and a few copies are left, so drop us a line if you wish one. The guest of honor at the party was Tex Cooper, the portrayer of Buffalo Bill in Hollywood. The boys riding for Cinnabar, Gerald & Ken Roberts and Louis Brooks were top-notchers throughout the rodeo. Kenneth is champion bull rider and Louis is the World's Champion Cowboy for 1943. Ken and Gerald Roberts with their wives, visited the Ranch before the rodeo. They are fine Western folks.

Your host ... C. J. Walter, who takes pleasure in teaching beginners to ride

On the Fire

When we started this edition of the News, we realized how much Allan is missed as he did all our publicity work in the past. In this first attempt we will do our best to bring the ranch news to you. We are proud to say all the Walter boys, excepting George have been in the Armed Forces. Let's hope they will all soon be home wrangling dudes again. Vern is in the Army Air Force, with a Bomber Group and has a New York Post Office address. We're expecting to hear from him from overseas soon. Allan is finishing manouevers at Camp Lee, Va. with the Quartermaster Corps. Stanley is stationed at Ft. Bragg, N. C. but right now is home celebrating the birth of his baby son who was born Sunday, the 23rd of January. Kenneth just received a discharge from the Canadian Army and Earl is in the Cavalry at Ft. Brown in Texas, but is hoping to be a paratrooper soon, so that makes us a four starrer. Blackie and Jake have been home on furlough and asked us to say hello to all their ranch friends through this News. Art Pritchard has an honorable discharge from the Army. He never lost the "Dude Ranch Fever", so we see him and Melly most every weekend. Bob Parker left the ranch to join the U.S.O. show entertaining the boys at camp, now is in the Navy. Irene and her enchanting daughter Connie Jeanette, spent the past months with Tom, who is Stable Sergeant for the Mounted Patrol of the Coast Guard in Philadelphia. Charlotte returned recently after spending two months with Allan in Petersburg, Va. Alyce and Stan managed a weekend in Washington this Spring. Peggy took charge of the office while Irene was away, so with the care of her husky son, George Earl, and the office work, had her hands full over the holidays. Curly returned from Alaska and has been helping out by driving the station wagon and entertaining the guests with his guitar playing and singing Western songs. The biggest catastrophe of the year happened when C. J. sold Doreen's trick horse "Chico" as she immediately took over Navajo, C. J.'s trick horse, however she and Maxine make a nice show with their trick riding and riding bareback on their pinto ponies. C. J. and Connie are still debating where to spend their vacation, it's a toss-up for Florida, or South Dakota, where we are planning a work Ranch, after the war. Adele Duke left the ranch this fall to join the WAC, and is now stationed in Oregon. We certainly appreciated the holly she sent us to decorate the dining room for the holidays. "Wildhorse" Peg McKay also in the WAC, is at Ft. Belvoir, Va. and has spent a few weekends with us. We were pleased to meet her buddies from camp, and hope to see them back again soon. C. J.'s sister, Clara, spent a nice vacation at Cinnabar, and after returning to Detroit couldn't stand the city life, so she too, joined the WAC. Herman Fredericks,

ee hour ride leaving the stables

Relaxing on our beautiful lake after a lon

our truck rider, rebought his beautiful pinto horse *Satan*, so is happy again. Herman was with us for two months last summer and now we can't get rid of him. It seems, by the look of his mare, *Penny*, he is going into the horse business too, as she is soon expecting a little one. Jean Wilson also was with us for two months helping Irene in the office. It was indeed a pleasure having her and proved a great help. Ivy Goodale who had charge of the store last summer is staying with her folks in Jersey City, but we hope to see her Dude Ranching again soon. Joe Breckenridge, a one-time bronc buster came East to help C.J. His Indian Sioux dance is a wild sight to see and a feature of our weekly initiations He has a surprise coming to the boys that usually bunk in Texas, as he has done quite a paint job up there. We are fortunate enough to have our famous cook, George Gilmore to give us plenty of good wholesome food. Charlotte's sister, Dotty has been up weekends helping out. She is our young "heartbreaker". Gloria & George Stumpp have been regular guests recently and are both proud horse owners. George decided to give up city life altogether and is on the ranch staff now. Jack Jordan, better known as Tex, a former ranch hand, has taken his horse *Noah* back to the city. Rumors are that he and Cecelia are planning on being married, good luck to you both! Ruth Bender spent a few weeks at the ranch with her folks and now is the proud owner of our Palamino trick horse, *Victory*. Dotty Mullen has been a frequent guest this winter, her latest love is *Bubbles*, a horse of course, and she sure likes "*Three of a kind or a full house.*" Eddie Drews and Jack Ahern, both of

For Reservations Write
CINNABAR RANCH
PEEKSKILL, N. Y.
Phone: Peekskill 402

★

or phone our New York office
RHinelander 4-7790

the Coast Guard have been up a few times, and it sure is good to see them. We have missed the old R.C.A. gang, Gus Anderson and Willis Chew are the only ones left. Hum Herdman roped himself a beautiful Spanish gal—we're still hoping to meet her. Hal Reidinger is seeing the world with the Coast Guard. Hank Zelner and John Golden are doing radio work for Uncle Sam. Walter Miller is in khaki, also Sam Pastorfield, who is in Alaska, and wonders why he ever paid us for skiing at the ranch. Ernest Clark has forsaken his beautiful "*Lady Belle*" for a Navy ship. Phyliss Clarke and Belle Rogers joined the W.A.C, and from the last reports are still together. Carolyn Golden, working in Washington, has been up for a few short visits. Allan Troxell is still traveling around. Rose Mandell is kept busy writing to a certain soldier. We'd love to mention all you folks who have been our guests, but there is a paper shortage. However, we do want you fellows and gals who are spread all over the globe to know that we really miss you!

——— Member ———
Eastern Dude Ranch Association.

ride

Birds-eye view of our Rodeo field

Honeymoon Cottage is Prospect for Newlyweds

Cinnabar, this past season, has been a regular Honeymoon Paradise, and the future is still romantic. We have plans to build an exclusive Honeymoon cottage on "Smooch Island," in the middle of the lake, so our honeymooners can have a bit of privacy. They will have their own boat for transportation, but I guess we will have to supply a lock for the boat, to fool the pranksters. Our lake was more popular than ever the past year, as more canoes and boats were on hand. The fishermen were fairly lucky, catching many pickerel and trout. It's a great sport but more fun than this is gathering around campfires in the evenings, frying the catch of the day.

Store News...

Here's the latest news of our Ranch Trading Post, which is being remodeled to include a bar to serve beer and sandwiches. We know you will be glad to hear that Connie will be the new storekeeper, so with her sweet smile will be able to "dude you out", as she has a complete supply of Western riding clothes, from boots and spurs to ten-gallon hats, along with souvenirs, keepsakes and novelties. The courtyard in front of the store, lit up with flood lights at night, is an active spot with guests showing-off their private horses, trick riding, etc, and with Buttercup, our pet donkey, bucking off anyone brave enough to get on. It seems there is a continuous show from dawn to midnight.

A WORD FROM OUR PRESIDENT, WHO IS IN THE ARMY

The Army makes one appreciate former everyday occurences especially when one thinks back to the pre-war days of home, car, week-end and vacation pleasures. Most G.I.'s have these uppermost in their minds and are determined to make the most of them when handed their Certificate of Service. Things naturally are missed more when not readily available. So—everyone who is doing his or her part at home, should take advantage of pleasures and liberties, which are a part of the reason we fight. Hope to see you all very soon.

ALLAN WAL

CINNABAR RANCH NEWS

AT CINNABAR

You thought that we were going home,
And you would have a rest,
But fate was kind and we won't roam
We'll still be little pests.
The food is good, the horses kind
And all is going well,
We love you folks at Cinnabar
And think you sure are swell.
We couldn't leave C.J. behind
Until he wins at poker,
Because we have been most unkind
And taken all his "doughka".
Connie with her sunny smile
And easy going ways,
We couldn't leave her to C. J.'s wiles
Because she always pays.
Curly plays a mean guitar
But he's awful temperamental,
He doesn't want to shine for us
And we're so sentimental.
To George, the mighty hunter
Who dishes out the corn,
He met the steer who was not "deer"
And now he is forlorn.
And now he plays the banjo
And drowns his sorrow in rye,
To hell with all the music,
We'd rather have more pie.
To Joe, the happy blacksmith
And Kate, his jolly wife
The next time he goes on a *toot*
She'll get him with a knife.
To Doreen and Maxine
Who play Jada Jada Jing,
C. J. will mow you down
With a bing, bing, bing!
To Joe the happy painter
With all the yarns to spin
Someday he'll tell a tall one
And boy will he cash in!
Peggy has a winning way
She's the one who helped us stay
We hope she won't rue the day
And make us bunk out in the hay.
Here ends our little story
Take it as you will,
For after all is said and done,
We still pay the bill.

Written and composed by the
"BRONC-BUSTIN DUDES"

Irene Mathers, Blanche Ade
and Emma Garribaldi

Square Dances and Rodeos Still Main Weekly Events

Our gala Saturday night Square Dances and Sunday Rodeos are still the highlights of the week. We wish to take this opportunity to thank Frank Steinrock for doing such a grand job announcing our Rodeos for us; Herman Fredericks for trick riding, and showing his horse "Satan"; Harry Keilly, Ed Nordsey, Paul Lafayette, Dick Chamberlain, Dave Wycoff and many others, for the active parts they and their horses played in making our Rodeos the success they have been. Our guests still look forward to taking part in the games and contests in the Rodeo. Each guest has a favorite Rodeo horse and takes pride in its appearance in the arena.

Holidays Still Celebrated the Western Way

We spent the holidays the old fashioned way, but we missed all the fellowes in the Service who are usually with us. Sure hope they all had a nice Christmas and a Happy New Year. Our New Year's week-end was a very successful one. The weather was perfect for both riding and skating. V for Vickery Lila, Lee Zoller, Eddie Drews, Dotty Mullen, Jack Aherne, Peg Fischer, Irene Mather, Blanch Ade, Garry Garribaldi, Gus Anderson, Willis Chew, Eileen and Nonie Malone, Jean Wilson, Tony Abreseze, Quinton Brown, Bob Anderson, Dotty Gunn, Charles Buttler, Jack Gerlitz, Irma Lugge, Herman Fredericks and Helen Asbury were a few of the oldtimers who helped us ring in the New Year. I'm sure they won't forget that week-end for awhile.

There are many more holidays coming—make arrangements and definite reservations early, to be sure you can be accommodated.

Famous Showman will add Color to Cinnabar this Coming Season

Wild Bill McCarthy is leaving his Medora horse ranch this Spring and is coming East to assist C. J. in handling the Rodeos and guests. He is one of the few ranchers left who has buffalo running loose on his range. Bill was with the Buffalo Bill Shows, 101 Shows, and has travelled through the United States and Europe. He sure will have many stories to keep the guests entertained. We met Bill in 1928 at Wood Mountain, Saskatchewan, and were surprised to see him last Summer when he came East with several carloads of horses for Steve Chase. We are looking forward to having him with us this Summer. He is bringing some of his outstanding rodeo stock with him.

CINNABAR RANCH NEWS

...URS OF A DUDE
...Y ONE OF THEM

The mounting feeling of excitement as the train stops at Peekskill, the wide, genial smile beneath the unmistakable cowboy hat and shyness disappearing under C.J.'s easy friendliness. The station wagon piled high with the afternoon's batch of guests; the thrill of seeing real country as the car turns off the highway into the cool, shaded road that winds past wooded hills, under a rustic arch to the wide, sunny "yard" and to the tiny town of Cinnabar, "Californias," inviting row of gay, little rooms; the picturesque barns with their round turreted silos, and the sheer green slopes of a mountain on the one side of the yard and the shimmer of a wide, blue lake below the windows of "Montana" on the other. Later the first meal in the big, friendly dining room; heartily welcome food served and eaten in an atmosphere of jollity; your sudden realization that everybody's calling everybody else by first names and chatting like old cronies. Games and the pleasant business of getting acquainted until it's time for sleep; sound sleep filled with dreams of the horse you'll ride tomorrow; the waking to the loud clamor of the "first bell"; breakfast over, the long, slow call from the barn "riders!" The big moment when the barn boss selects a horse for you and swings you up to the saddle; the impatient wait while cinches and stirrups are all given a final check. The comparing of notes "What horse have you got?" "Oh, he's a good ride, I had him yesterday" "I always ask for my favorite, Teatrader, Bubbles, Montana or Chocolate". Then that perfectly marvelous sensation you always have when a good horse is moving under you; the beautiful, gay sight of the long row of brightly clad riders moving against dark shadowed woods; the pause to water the horses in the brook; the "ride"; now a walk, now a lope, to Cimarron's "Western Town". A rest and a drink at the "Last Chance" and back to Cinnabar by a different route, through woods and over hills and across little running streams. The dinner you devour with gusto; the sun filling the yard, where you sit and watch through half-closed eyes while a cowboy shows ambitious dudes how to spin a rope; the sense of living in an utterly new world, but the feeling you've lived there long enough to belong. The surge of ambition returning when one of your new-found friends suggests a swim; the cool, clear water; tiny "Smooch Island"; the boats and the diving board; the delicious sensation of the sun warming you as you lie on the float, soaking it in. Supper and the feeling that there is nothing in the world so marvelous as a good meal after an active day. Full of life, browned and healthy, promising yourself that you'll come back! For there can be no one-time visitor to Cinnabar. They always come again, and again.

In the Dinner Bell

Spend your Weekends at Cinnabar — but BUY WAR BONDS FIRST!

Return Postage Guaranteed

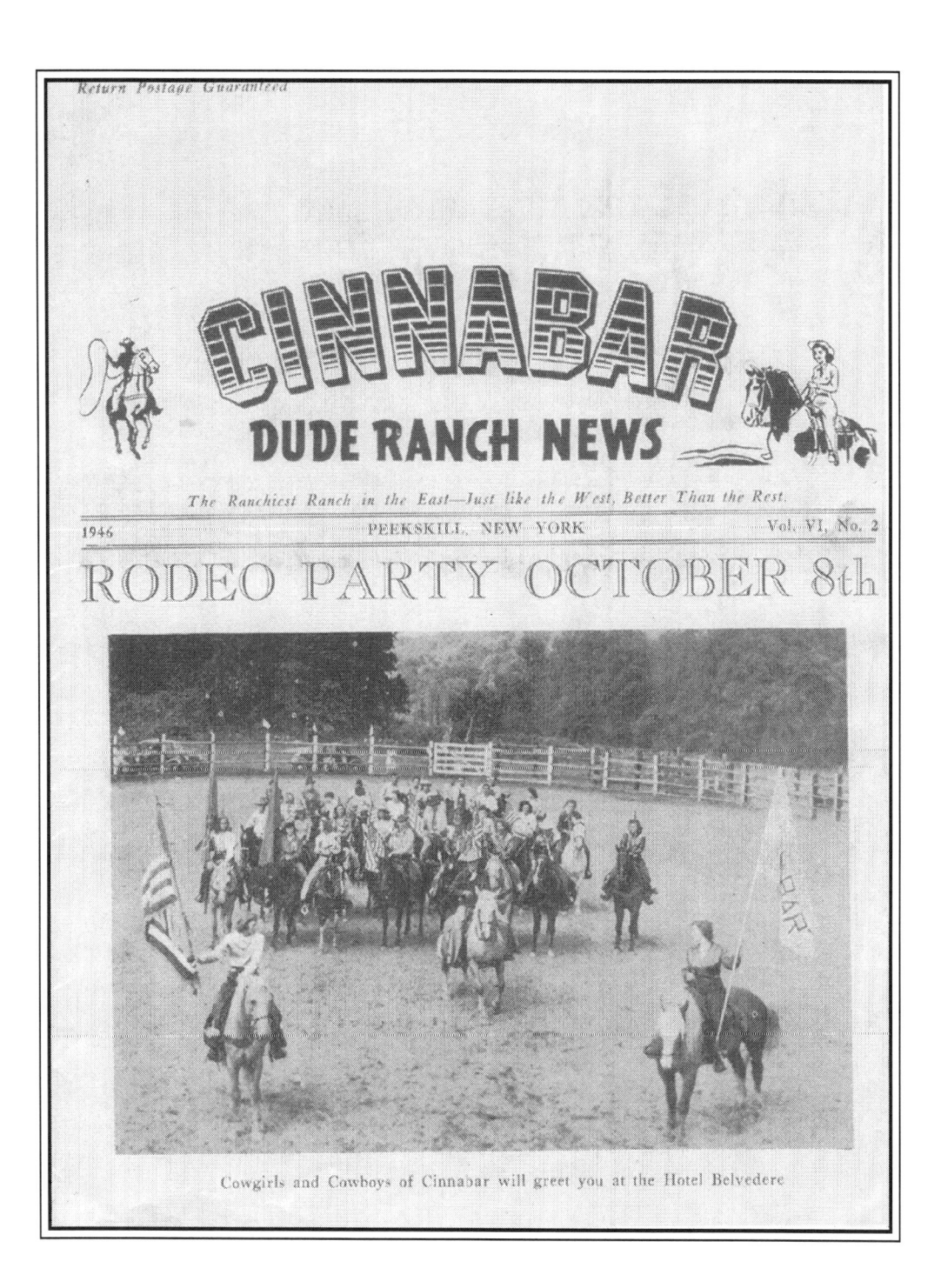

CINNABAR
DUDE RANCH NEWS

The Ranchiest Ranch in the East—Just like the West, Better Than the Rest.

1946   PEEKSKILL, NEW YORK   Vol. VI, No. 2

RODEO PARTY OCTOBER 8th

Cowgirls and Cowboys of Cinnabar will greet you at the Hotel Belvedere

to Renew Ranch Friendships

HARRY TOMPKINS AND EARL WALTER TO COMPETE IN MADISON SQUARE GARDEN EVENTS

For the seventh consecutive year guests and friends of Cinnabar Ranch will hold their annual get-togther at the Hotel Belvedere and Madison Square Garden on Tuesday, October 8, 1946.

Fun, frolic and an entirely enjoyable evening is always the motto of these parties. Judging from the response already received this year's party should be the equal of any held in past years.

At the party you will have the pleasure of meeting participants of the rodeo such as Gene Autry and others. Schedules will be arranged to have our own cowboys, Earl Walter and Harry Tompkins compete in their favorite events that night.

Only 300 of the best seats have been reserved (space at the Hotel Belvedere being limited) so we have adopted a policy of the first reservations received to get

C. J. Walter and His Six Sons Say Hello Once More

Make your reservations! now

WHAT TO DO:

Write to Lila or Jean at the ranch office stating the number of tickets you wish reserved. Your friends and relatives are cordially invited. Enclose your check or money order for the total amount ($8.50 each reservation). Make remittances to Cinnabar Ranch, Peekskill, N. Y.

Upon receipt of your reservation, spaces will be held for you and acknowledgement immediately sent. Your tickets will be held until October 8, when ranch personnel will surrender them as you arrive.

Four p. m. will be the start of activities for the night. Souvenir gifts from the ranch to each person will make this a memorable occasion. Rooms will be available to deposit coats, etc., and to change to ranch clothing if you wish.

After saying hello to all the folks you know from the ranch, dinner will be announced. The finest food available will be served in the manner deemed most efficient.

The Grand Entry at Madison Square Garden will be at 8:30 sharp. This is just across the street and our special section will be waiting for us to watch the biggest and most famous rodeo in the world. There we will watch our own boys compete in the toughest competition possible.

After the rodeo, we return to the ballroom of the Hotel Belvedere for a real old-time square dance to the tunes of a top notch cowboy band. During the dance drawing will be held for the winners of four free weekends at Cinnabar during October or November, two of the finest months of the year at the ranch.

Your ticket to the rodeo, supper, souvenirs, free drawing for weekends at the ranch, the dance and entertainment are all included in the low cost of $8.50 per person. This is your chance to see the rodeo and meet your friends of the ranch at the same time.

Dress is optional. Many will come in ranch clothes and we will also have a dressing room for those wishing to change.

FOR AN ENJOYABLE EVENING WITH FRIENDS, MAKE RESERVATIONS NOW!

WHAT IT MEANS...

E. D. R. A. means the Eastern Dude Ranchers Association which was formed in 1940 by a group of dude ranch owners to uphold the high standards of conduct, riding and facilities expected by ranch guests.

Whenever you see the E. D. R. A. sign you will know that particular ranch has been approved by the central committee and is your guarantee of a good vacation or weekend. Cinnabar is a charter member of the Eastern Dude Ranchers Association.

CINNABAR RODEO

Rodeos held each week at the ranch found many guests taking part in the various events. Bea DeForest gamely rode the first bull out of the chutes on August 10. Doreen Walter decided that trick riding would be easier than riding bulls so she has been concentrating on this phase of rodeo life.

Over 30,000 saw the rodeo in Union City, N. J. which was sponsored by the Police Department as a benefit for children. One little boy, hurt during his hurry to reach the rodeo, was visited by the rodeo hands and has something to remember for many years. August meant five full days at the Hudson Valley Exposition and September rodeos were held at New Brunswick, N. J. and Danbury, Connecticut.

"C. J." expressed thanks to all the boys who returned from service and made these rodeos the outstanding successes they were. We all hope to see much more of them in the future.

Most of the pictures in this Dude Ranch News were taken by Dorothy Gunn who has spent the whole summer at the ranch photographing guests and all ranch activities.

It is a familiar sight to see Cinnabar's orange and green 12-horse trailer pulling out loaded with bucking horses to fulfill a rodeo contract someplace in Connecticut, New York or New Jersey.

Rodeos were held at the ranch each week but enough extra time was found to contract for shows in Danbury, Connecticut, Union City, N. J., New Brunswick, N. J., Woodstock, N. Y. and at the Hudson Valley Exposition at Peekskill, N. Y.

C. J. Walter and his son Earl work together promoting these shows. The square dance team is made up of the following girls on their favorite horses, Dorothy Shaaf, Maxine Walter, Dorothy Cooper, and Doreen Walter. Doreen also competes in the trick riding events. Joe De Filippis and his wonder horse "Smoky" take care of the feature trick act.

Other performers deserving of mention are Pat Maellaro, trick riding on his horse Brutus; Jack Andrews with his trained Brahma bull "Henry"; Tom Brown and Bill Stanfield with their acts from Calico Ranch, Woodstock, N. Y.; Cliff Finnerty, better known as "Finnegan," Bill Cooney, for taking care of the rodeo stock, Ed Burkhart, for his devotion to maimed or sick horses; Paul Lafayette, for his advice and able judging at the shows; George Walter, for his entry into most events; Augie Bartholdi, for his trick riding; "Hap" Pilz, for his able clowning and act with 'Sara"; Jackie Lafayette, for his horse and trick riding; "Chesty" Tyler for his singing and strumming on the guitar; Bob Layman, for his able M. C. chores and clear voice over the PA system; Harry Tompkins, for his professional rides on steers and bareback horses; Stan Walter, Blackie Miozzi and Art Pritchard for their untiring care of the entire ranch string of horses.

Rides With Stan Walter Are Always Popular

As the days, weeks and months go by they leave us with a store of never-to-be forgotten memories and a host of friends who, we hope, will find time to visit us time and again in the future. It gives us a great feeling when we know you folks have had a good time at the ranch and will be back to see us.

During the past few years a great number of you men were graduated from the Merchant Marine Academy at Kings Point, Long Island. This spring a number from each graduating class decided Cinnabar was the place for their last good time together. They had a good time and it's a pleasure to get their cards and letters from various parts of the world. Thomas and Steiner, being instructors, have had more chance to get up during the summer. . . . Our well-known "Mexican" gang will be up again after Labor Day. They like the off seasons just like a lot of our other guests. It will be good to greet them again . . . After three full years of overseas duty, Lem Leavitt spent several weeks with us but seemed a little lost without the rest of the gang. He will be back when he can roundup Al Ghirardi, Al Birra and Sam Pastorfield. Maybe they can make it for the rodeo party . . . When the phone rings during the week we have expectations of hearing the voice of Walter Scott. It has happened quite often this year and it is always a pleasure to say "Come right up". . . . The two Kays, O'Neill and Eberling, if not at home on weekends, are probably spending their time and money at the ranch . . . Freddie Pomadowski has the ideal vacation set-up; he seems to have three two-week periods each year, and best part of it is he spends them at the ranch . . . Everett "Tiny" Titus and Minerva Ebbe spent a couple of weeks at the ranch eyeing each other, went home, are being married in October. The best of luck to you and it means a free weekend at the ranch . . . Lila Vickery our efficient Girl Friday in the office, was seen by Harry Brittain, was conquered and is now Mrs. Brittain. June was the time and both are working at the ranch . . . Jean and Harry Youngberg celebrated their eleventh wedding anniversary at the ranch in August Jean is working in the office with Lila and Harry manages to get up several days during the week to entertain us with his guitar and voice . . . Harry Conover, the Cover Girl man, has his own horse at the ranch but cannot give him as much time as he would like. His business keeps him on the the go most of the time but it is always good to see Candy and Harry drive into the yard . . . Rose Mandell, Vic Alpi, Lee Zoller, Al Meyers, John Hogan, Lorraine Kitenplon, Eleanor Hughes, Francis Pantaleo, Fran and Pat Campbell are "regulars" whose arrival is always welcomed . . . Mary Lewicki of the Mortha Owen Travel Agency in New York City has been up several times this year. Guests booked by the agency are too numerous to mention. . . Many of our early season guests were those just returned from overseas duty. Among these were "Wildhorse" Peg McKay, Bob Knapp and Jerry Lipman . . . We hope all their futures are shaping up as expected . . . Ann and Tony DeLuca spent their honeymoon at Cinnabar, liking it well enough to spend another week later. Other honeymoon couples at the ranch were Louise and Mike Trulis, Mr. and Mrs. Norman Watson, Mr. and Mrs. Arthur LaRue, Mr. and Mrs. Herbert Klein, Mr. and Mrs. Roy Hoffman, Mr. and Mrs. Dan Rodgers, Mr. and Mrs. Fred Brittain, Mr. and Mrs. Edward Rogers, Mr. and Mrs. Lamberto Cacciotte, Mr. and Mrs. Joseph Pinter, Jr., Mr. and Mrs. Clinton Jordan, Mr. and Mrs. Joseph Scazzero, and Mr. and Mrs. William Cooper. . .

"Rodeo Queens" Dorothy Cooper, Dorothy Schaaf, Doreen Walter and Maxine Walter have had a busy year with their ranch and rodeo work.

On the Fire

We're all enjoying a well-earned rest after a busy season. Peggy suffered a painful hand injury just before Christmas but it is fast repairing.

Earl Walter and Harry Tompkins represented Cinnabar Ranch in Colonel Eskew's Rodeo Show last year; their circuit included such widely separated cities as Philadelphia and Montreal. In Montreal Earl broke his leg while bulldogging. It was a tough break for him as he had counted on being a contestant in the Boston and Madison Square Garden shows.

Besides the prolific Walters, the ranch help now includes George Gilmore, Ed Burkhart, Harry Tompkins, Bill Vogel, Lila Vickery, and Dorothy Cooper. In addition we are looking for the early return of Blackie Miozzi and Jake Kornhaus from service and Artie Pritchard expects to rejoin the gang. It's a swell ranch family.

Bill Daly set some sort of a record when he came up for a weekend and stayed five weeks . . . he was recuperating from army service. Other ranch guests just before we closed for the winter included Al Meyers, Mr. and Mrs. Andy Kornylak with their baby Tommy, Gus Anderson, Lee Zoller, Rose Mandell, Chuck Mitchell and Peggy Crawford.

John Hogan was up just before Christmas—he has been a real friend to Cinnabar, having helped us this past summer to clear trail, lead rides and call square dances. This spring John plans to come up and blaze several new trails. And John, that Christmas present sure hit the spot.

We are glad to report that Blanche Ade is back at work after a severe illness. Bill Vogel with his famous goatee has been a powerhouse helping to put on the rodeo shows and taking care of the stock, not to mention his really fine painting.

The last weekend of the season was devoted to cementing our good neighborly relations with the "Mexicans". We expect to see them all again early in the new season.

We had a letter from WAC Betty Heisler written while she was on furlough at home. She plans to return to Germany for a year as a civilian.

Dottie Thunhorst was the last guest of the season—she broke in our new appaloosa horse.

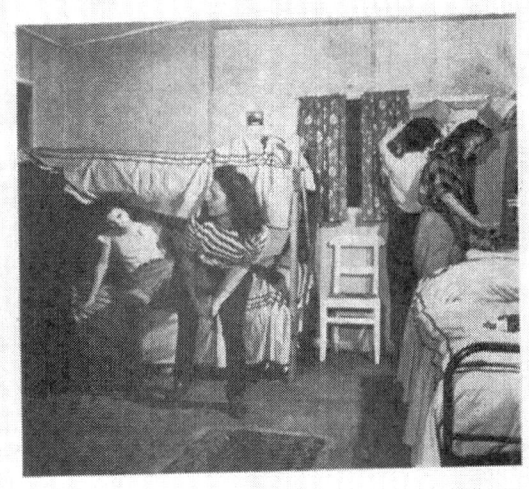

Four Cinnabarettes preparing for an evening of Square Dancing after a busy day of riding and swimming.

Cinnabar will open for the 1946 Season on March first. Make yo[ur] Reservations now for March Accommodations.

TRADING POST EXPANDS

Cinnabar's Trading Post, always a popular rendezvous for guests during the afternoon and evening, will present a new appearance this season. A lunch counter will be installed which will serve coffee and light lunches in the evenings.

A large stock of western clothing, horse equipment and novelties will be on the shelves of the store. You will be able to fit yourself out from head to toe in western duds right on the ranch.

Just off from the store and lunch counter a large dance floor will be constructed. It is expected that the floor will receive hard usage from guests waiting for the ride to go out or for the dinner gong to ring.

C. J. GOES WEST

In search of fifty new horses to add to Cinnabar's string and for rodeo purposes C. J. Walter left for Arizona and other points west shortly after New Years. Accompanying him was his son Earl. During the five week trip they plan to visit many western operating ranches in search of new ideas applicable to our ranch as well as replacements for horses sold last fall.

C. J. expects to return rested and ready for six months "work" — managing rodeos, quarter horse racing, renewing old acquaintances and making new friends. It's a great life and C. J. thrives on it.

CULTURE DIVISION

A Cinnabar dude on a ride
Had mounted from the right side
The steed made a leap
Left the dude in a heap
In this case right was wrong the wretch cried.
        BMW

The Virginia Reel — ever popular at Cinnab[ar's] frequent square dances.

FLASH!!

We learn as presstime nears that Allan Wai[te] has just returned from eighteen months service [in] the Persian Gulf Command. Awaiting him [at] Cinnabar is his lovely wife Charlotte and Allan, [Jr.] a husky sixteen month old boy whom Allan [has] never seen. Welcome home Allan.

For Reservations
WRITE

CINNABAR RANCH
PEEKSKILL, NEW YORK

Phone: Peekskill 402

MEMBER
EASTERN DUDE RANCH ASSOCIATION

RODEOS

Cinnabar is looking forward to one of its biggest rodeo seasons this year at home, and on the road. C. J. is now out West selecting another load of broncos and steers, and if they are anywhere near what we had last year, there'll be plenty of thrills and spills. More novelty events will be featured this coming season so that the guests will be able to take part in our Sunday rodeos.

The ranch was complimented when such personalities as Ken and Gerald Roberts, Lobo Larsen, Ike Rude, Ken Boen and several others paid us a visit to look over the ranch and our stock. Chief Bear Shield, a bronc rider from Dakota, paid C. J. a visit, and naturally we saw a resemblance. Speaking of rodeo personalities, our own Harry Tompkins did very well at Madison Square and Boston.

The Eastern Aircraft workers held their annual picnic at our rodeo field one Sunday in July. The usual Cinnabar weather didn't hold true this day, and our show was given in a sea of mud... even the rain didn't stop us, and a good time was had by all. We wound up our rodeo season with a three day show at the Peekskill Armory for the Hudson Valley Exposition. This year we plan to show a full week at Peekskill and at Danbury plus many one day stands.

In the photo Bill Vogel assisted by lovely cowgirl Joan Fell is rounding up steers for the Sunday rodeo.

"FOTOCREST" Studio Announces Opening

Commencing in May you will be able to take home with you a picture of yourself and your favorite "pony". Dorothy (Dottie) Gunn is resigning her position with Abraham & Straus where she worked in advertising photography, in order to open her own studio "FOTOCREST" to be located near Cinnabar Ranch. Always interested in horses and dude ranching, she plans to specialize from now on in glamour pictures of you guests and your horses, action rodeo shots, and outdoor fashion work. Dividing her time between Cinnabar and Cimarron, with occasional trips to nearby ranches, should keep Dot a pretty busy gal this summer. Here's wishing her best of luck in her new venture!

CIMARRON and CINNABAR MAIL POUCH

SEPTEMBER, 1940   PEEKSKILL, NEW YORK   Vol. 2, No. 2

Dude Ranches Have Record Season

Cinnabar Receives Instant Approval

By VERN WALTER

Th first all-day rain since Decoration Day affords us an opportunity to pause and reflect on the happenings of a busy season.

The gay voices coming from the Game Room where there is a Ping Pong Tournament to decide the inter-ranch champion, who will receive a ranch prize of a pair of cowboy or cowgirl boots, besides all entry monies, lets one know that there is no gloom on dude ranches even during inclement weather. All seem grateful that the horses who have so faithfully performed their duties this summer, are getting their first holiday of the season.

It has always been our contention that people who go to dude ranches are primarily interested in riding, so we have provided horses enough at both ranches to assure everyone a full two or three hour ride each day, with enough extra to allow each horse a certain period of rest without declaring a general horse holiday, at the expense of our guests.

The wisdom of our policy is borne out by the record crowds that have *(continued Page 4 column 1)*

Rodeo Round-up Parties October 16th, 23rd

Mike Hastings and Fritz Truan to Represent Ranches in Garden Rodeo

The annual fall rodeo roundup party will be held in two sections this fall to accommodate the large number of guests and their friends who are expected to attend.

The program for the parties is as follows:

Dinner and Get-Together at the Hotel Belvedere (headquarters for the rodeo contestants and just across the street from Madison Square Garden) from five to eight P.M., rodeo, (first 200 requests receive box seats) at 8:30—then, immediately following the show, Ray Whitley and his Bar Six Cowboys of screen and radio fame, will play for dancing at the Belvedere where you will meet Gene Autry and many other stars of the rodeo at our own private party. Movies of the ranch will be shown before and after the rodeo.

The tariff, including a $3.85 box, (we have been allotted 200 boxes and an additional 100 $3.35 arena seats,) chicken dinner at Hotel Belvedere, souvenir and dance to Ray Whitley's band, is $5.00. The party October 16th will be sponsored by Cimarron, October 23rd by Cinnabar. Don't fail to attend at least one of these gay affairs. There's fun aplenty to be had and if you've never attended a World's Championship Rodeo, you have a special treat in store for you. AND DON'T FORGET OUR OWN MIKE HASTINGS WILL BE IN THERE RIDING FOR CIMARRON AND CINNABAR—SO C'MON AND LET'S HELP CHEER HIM ALONG! But remember this, the first 200 requests receive box seats and there are only 100 additional seats available, so pick a date and send your check or money order at least one week in advance for the show you wish to attend. Make checks payable to *Cimarron-Cinnabar Rodeo Party* and mail to Dude Ranches, Peekskill, New York. Don't forget to specify the party or parties you wish to attend. Your tickets will be given to you at the Hotel Belvedere the night of the party. Dress-informal.

Return Postage Guaranteed
DUDE RANCHES
PEEKSKILL, N. Y.

Sec. 562, P. L. & R.
U.S. Postage
PAID
New York, N. Y.
Permit No. 1578

LABOR DAY WEEKEND GAY EVENT
Dance, Rodeo, Movies, Highlights

In spite of threatening weather, a carnival air of good fellowship prevailed throughout a weekend of old-fashioned barn dancing, riding, Wild West Movies, and our own Wild West Rodeo on Sunday. Doc Ross and Jim Gunter were color bearers in the parade and, as usual, Herb Moll made an especially fine showing with his high-school horse "Lady Belle" whom he has so expertly trained. And, of course, our own MIKE HASTINGS was right in there "throwing the bull" and that's literally speaking, too! Bob Layman made a nice ride on his steer and while Wilbur Chase was thrown from "Little Snake," it's no disgrace because he has thrown the best of them! All saddle bronc riders managed to stay on for the regulation ten seconds. Earl Walter rode "Steamboat," Wilbur Chase "Black Flash" and Chuck Connors "Brown Bomber." Vern Walter started the rough stuff by fanning his bronc until the whistle blew, having the biggest difficulty in unloading. Paul Laune gave us an added bucking horse event when he spurred "Show Boy" too far back in an over-zealous attempt to make time roping his calf. By the cheers from the crowd on the rails, it was evident that the rodeo was well run by C. J. Walter and you can bet it was well announced by our genial guest Frank Steinrock. The balloon fight (which gets rougher and rougher) between guests of Cimarron and Cinnabar was declared a "draw." It was heartening to hear a man remark after the show that he had recently returned from the Southwest where he had witnessed a rodeo put on by three big dude ranches and ours was more spectacular then theirs.

City Gals Rather Square Dance

Possibly it's like the women's styles that, at times, draw on yester-year for their fashion, that makes the dudes of today prefer the old folk dance of yesterday, the old-fashioned square dance . . . Speaking of styles, Mary Laune says this year's women's styles are being influenced by dude ranches; mebbe so, but I gotta see how a pair of chaps and a typewriter look together.

"Holding-up the Mail at Cimarron's Western-town"

Dude Ranches Gain in Popularity
Many guests just learning to ride

The big trend to dude-ranching that has been so evident this season has brought with it a problem for the alert rancher in the large number of guests who have never ridden before. Unless care is taken, a beginner can get mighty sore and lame and soon become discouraged, but we have found that with a little patience, and a systematic plan of teaching, in a few days, rank beginners are enjoying a gallop along with the old-timers. We are careful to grade our riders and keep them in a group and on horses suited to their speed.

Hunting Season Ahead

Falling leaves bring on the urge to go hunting which reminds us to see about that shack at the end of Cod Pond Flow in the Adirondacks and we are wondering if anybody would like to go along. The season is November 1st to the 30th and the deer are plentiful in this out-of-the-way spot. Weekly all expense trips are planned. Fifty dollars covers all expenses for one week; transportation from the Ranch, guides, etc.

After that outing from routine ranch affairs, we must hustle with the ski trails and the new toboggan slide to be built on to the ice of Lake Corral for we're going to have a housefull of happy winter sports fans this season.

Frontier Town Popular

Western Town has been the center of gay life at Cimarron this season. It has provided the added bit of activity needed for this secluded spot so far away from everything. I doubt if one can realize just how secluded we are without seeing for one's self because, invariably, guests will remark that they can't believe they are only fifty miles from New York City; but when you realize we actually have five miles of unbroken range between the two ranches, you can see it's a little bit wild.

Excellent Ranch Horses

The remuda of 80 fine saddle horses used on the Cimarron-Cinnabar Ranches is not only the largest string on any Eastern Ranch but also of a finer quality. Practically all were shipped from Wyoming and Montana this year and were picked for their easy-riding qualities as well as their looks. Possibly it won't be the first one you ride but you are certain to find one of this large number that suits you to a tee.

Contest Winners

First place in the brand contest was awarded jointly to Marion Borton and William Planck Thomas who also submitted the name "Sundown" for the new guest cottage. Marion Flood offered the name "Western Town" for our new town and "Silver Saddle Trading Post" was sent in by Billy Berneko. How's about collecting Bill and Billy?

DUDE RANCHES HAVE RECORD SEASON

(continued from Page 1)

been guests of the new Cinnabar Ranch and the enlarged Cimarron Ranch this season; and also by the large percentage of guests who return time and time again. We now go a step farther in offering *exclusive use of a saddle horse* from Monday through Friday at Cimarron, and the riding at Cinnabar will be increased to the half-day schedule for the Fall Season.

Cinnabar Opens On Decoration Day

It was on May 10th, that final negotiations were made that added the beautiful estate of Stuyvesant Fish to the Cimarron Ranch Family.

Less than three weeks to put the buildings in readiness for Decoration day—true, it had been operated as a ranch before, but there was much to do. All rooms had to be decorated and draperies hung . . . furniture, rugs and carpets purchased, plumbing to install and a kitchen to get in operation. Also, there were horses to buy and saddles, bridles and blankets to go with them. By the dint of hard work and long hours, everything was in readiness for the opening and a capacity crowd gave the new lay-out instant approval.

Cimarron also had its opening of the new Sundown Guest Cottage increasing the ranch capacity to 72 guests.

The summer weeks have been a bee-hive of activity—right from Monday's instruction rides, guests' initiation, hayrides, mid-week barn dances, picnics, pack-trips, camp-fires, Saturday night square dances, to our popular Sunday afternoon rodeos.

Looking Forward

Now we must turn to what lies ahead. The round-up parties will require a lot of attention. Sue will want to sit with Sally, and we, of course, know that Bill's girl is Mary, etc., etc.—but all the effort is pleasure to we who labor on the details when we are rewarded with beaming smiles and hardy handclasps at our annual reunions.

The Fall Season causes one to long, momentarily, for the warm summer days but the beauty of the color in the mountains soon makes one proclaim it the nicest time of the year and especially so for horseback riding. The horses feel snappy and because the crowds are not so large, all day rides with lunch packed on the saddle are the rule.

Birdseye View of Beautiful Cinnabar Ranch With Lake Corral in the Background

Mike Hastings
By ALLAN WALTER

Any story about Cinnabar must, of necessity, center about Mike Hastings, corral boss and the outstanding personality of the ranch. The horse has been Mike's business every day of his life. The experience gained by association with Colonel Johnson's Famous Shows, the winning of many calf-roping events and the World's Champion Steer-Wrestling Trophy, has made him one of the most outstanding Western horsemen living today. Incidentally, Mike was one of the originators of the dangerous sport of steer wrestling. The numerous guests who took their first horseback ride at the ranch will always remember Mike mounting his horse "Old Dog," cussing a good natured streak, heading out for one of the numerous trails surrounding the ranch, and returning with them as riders instead of beginners. And who couldn't help but love this grand old man of the West?

Hoot Gibson Ranch Visitor

Hoot Gibson, famous cowboy star of screen and rodeo, was a recent visitor to the ranch in quest of horses for his Wild West Show which is now touring the East.

Grace Miller takes the prize for prolonged stays . . . stopped in for a weekend and stayed a month. Wish you could stay a year, Grace, and congratulations on winning the ping-pong tournament! C. J. says he's sure glad you won because he's been trying to get you to buy cowboy boots for three years!

Eleanor Smith of Philly, Bee Beebe, Roger Main and Rusty O'Connell are other four-week visitors. Oh yes, I almost forgot Sonia ("heart-break") Dorosh. We are always glad to see the old timers. Al Ghirardi and his pal, Birra, have been the "steadies" as have Joe Handman, Paula Ernst, Butch Gilbert, Rose and Gene Civetta, Merv Stratton, Joyce Buford, Ranger VanKleeck and many others. Sam Pastorfield will put his boat in dry dock soon . . . we hope! I've a yen to see that O'Neil gang often again; in fact, do you know it is mighty hard to find fault with any of our dudes or dudettes? I don't think there has been one all summer who wasn't regular . . . We'll be anxious to hear all about the Western Dude Ranch trip of Marion Flood and Karen Wallen. We envy you! School calls Ingrid home. We miss you, Ingie, and Irene, too!

Pack Trip Loses Horses

There was no joy in camp one recent morning when a group who had packed into Lake Clearwater up on the Fahnestock Reservation for an overnight stay awoke to find that their horses had strayed away in the night; but, lucky for them, a farmer some miles away caught them and put them in his pasture. Bob said he guessed they just could not stand his singing any longer.

NEW YORK OFFICE: 155 EAST 42nd STREET - PHONE MUrray Hill 6-8588

CIMARRON and CINNABAR MAIL POUCH

Ranch Programs Announced

Cinnabar will close for the season November 1st. The week-end following the Rodeo Round-up party on October 23rd will mark the season's closing.

Many guests are planning an extended week-end coming to the Ranch direct from the Round-up Party, Wednesday night. The ranch will re-open on May 15th, 1941 with a bigger and better programme in store for you.

Cimarron Ranch never closes. The fall season will feature riding. Exclusive use of saddle horse from Monday to Saturday at no increase in rates. If you really like to ride, come up to Cimarron this fall. Long rides in the warm sun amid foliage so beautiful that it will amaze you, are in store for you. Pack a lunch and let's go see just what really is over that last ridge of mountains! And don't forget to plan your winter vacation at Cimarron. Skiing, skating, tobogganing and, of course, riding. Horses are sharp shod and the country is all yours.

Dont Miss the Rodeo Parties Oct. 16th & 23rd

Dudes Provide Many Laughs For Cowboys

"Riding drag" in ranch parlance means "bringing up the rear." Recently, I met a Cinnabar Ride on the trail and found a little gal trailing quite a way behind. I asked her if she were "riding drag" and she replied, that she did not know what his name was but that he was terrible!

* * *

One "doodle-bug" wanted to know who held the bull dogs while Mike "bull-dogged the steer."

* * *

Jack Roth, Cinnabar Jack-of-all-trades, was caught in the arms of a fair dudette by a former guest who exclaimed, "Why, Jack! I thought you were a shy boy" . . . Jack replied that he was shy, shy three gals for tonight!

Luxurious Steam-heated Accommodations Await You at the Ranches

HOLIDAY TARIFF SCHEDULE:

	Dorm.	½ Double Bedroom	½ Twin Bedroom	Private Room
Columbus Day, October 12th (2 days)	$13.00	$14.00	$15.00	$16.00
Armistice Day, November 11th (3 days)	18.00	19.50	21.00	22.00
Thanksgiving Day, Novmber 28th (4 days)	24.00	26.00	28.00	30.00
Christmas, December 25th (1 day)	9.00	10.00	11.00	12.00
New Year's, January 1st (1 day)	10.00	11.00	12.00	13.00

To avoid disappointments send a deposit on your reservation NOW!
NEW YORK OFFICE: 155 EAST 42nd STREET — PHONE MUrray Hill 6-8588

1944 Madison Square Garden Rodeo Brochure Ad – Centerfold Left

BETTY CULLY, assistant and LU WALTER, manager — pinchhitting for Vern.

MIKE HASTINGS, world famous cowboy and Cimarron's corral boss.

Cimarron's Western Town is the talk of the East. You've seen it pictured in Look, Spot, P. M., Liberty, Picture World, etc.

N RANCH
NEW YORK

Real Western Town.

Miles of trails in beautiful country.

50 Horses, one for every type rider.

Write for illustrated booklet.

Fast and frequent train service from N. Y. C.

Parties and dancing, movies and hayrides provide evening entertainment amid an air of good fellowship.

R OF THE EAST-
H ASSOCIATION

UY WAR BONDS
AND STAMPS

Guests take part or look on and enjoy the Sunday Rodeos. Top hands of Range and Rodeo are here to entertain you.

Saving Gas—The stage coach provides a new thrill in transportation. Cimarron offers the best of the West to you.

Now on Hand
AT ITS
PRE-WAR BEST!

With its rare basic *whiskies drawn from precious pre-war stocks, Three Feathers is skillfully blended with the choicest of American grain neutral spirits. Three Feathers — at its pre-war best—is deservedly termed "First Among Fine Whiskies". Try it today!

40% straight whiskey, 60% grain neutral spirits. 12½% straight whiskey 5 years old, 12½% straight whiskey 6 years old, 15% straight whiskey 7 years old.

1944 Madison Square Garden Rodeo Brochure Ad – Centerfold Right

Sketches of C.J. Walter by guests at the ranches

Dottie Cooper, Dottie Schaaf, Doreen Walter, Mackie Walter

Adios

We hope you have enjoyed these memories
as much as we have had sharing them.

~ Irene and Doreen

Made in the USA
Lexington, KY
11 February 2013